The History of the Hopi From Their Origins In Lemuria

Oswald White Bear Fredericks
Kaih Khristé King

First Edition

© 2009 Kaih Khristé King

All profits from this book, any other publications, art pieces and posters produced by Ms. King and Ms. Radiance go directly to The King's Bridge Ministries, a nonprofit 501(c)(3) corporation. The corporation holds all copyrights. Your tax-free donations are deeply appreciated.

Cover art by Blanche Radiance

For a brochure of Ms. Radiance's posters, or information on Ms. King's presentations and her schedule and for permission to print or quote from this book contact the publisher.

Published by The King's Bridge
Mailing Address: P. O. Box 78541
Shreveport, LA 71137
Phone: 310-433-0941
www.thekingsbridge.com

ISBN 978-0-9792099-7-0

Printed in the United States of America

Table of Contents

Foreword by Michael Lightweaver

Part One
Custodians of the Ancient Way
Naomi and White Bear

Part Two
As the Old Ones Told it

Part Three
The Third World

Part Four
Custodians of the Ancient Way
Naomi and White Bear

Part Five
Hopi Legend

Part Six
The Hopi Point of View

The History of the Hopi
From Their Origins
In Lemuria

Cover Art
Blanche Radiance

Editing
Sedona Junaid
Barbara Brown

Technical Assistance
Ken Nikolai

Foreword

Prior to my first trip to Sedona, Arizona in 1990, a friend suggested that, if possible, I meet with White Bear, the Hopi Elder who was the source for much of the information in the Book of The Hopi which was published in 1969.

At the time I was deeply involved in the Native American spiritual path and learning all I could about the teachings of the ancestors of this land. I was forewarned that his wife, Naomi, served as a guardian – that very few were able to pass and actually speak with White Bear.

A few weeks before the trip, I phoned and Naomi answered and in her very direct manner, I was pummeled with a score of questions as to who I was, what I wanted, etc. In mid-conversation there was a switch. She softened and said she liked my southern accent – and she trusted me and would be happy to have me visit.

The visit took place but most of it was with Naomi – a delightful Elder that I instantly bonded with. She gave me some insights and history about what they had had to deal with over the years; both from their own people and curious white folks. I began to understand her caution and reservation as she spilled out various betrayals they had experienced.

Before I left, she handed me an unpublished manuscript which she had personally typed for White Bear. It was his story of the history of the Hopi from their origins in Lemuria. I was taken aback. I was a virtual stranger to her. I suggested two or three other people who were writers or publishers that could actually bring it to print but she insisted that I take it. Finally I did with a sense of guardianship. A few years later White Bear and Naomi both passed on and the manuscript sat on my bookshelf.

Realizing the value of the information and the possibility that I might have the only copy, I made a few additional copies and sent them to trusted friends to keep.

Then in the autumn of 2008, the manuscript became restless. Apparently the time had arrived for it to 'come out.' Consequently, I had it typed into a Word document and, following Guidance, sent it to my friend Kaih Khristé King. She, White Bear and Naomi were good friends and Kaih was actually much closer to the Bears than I was.

Kaih knows I'm fine with changing the script or having her edit/rewrite it if she feels it necessary to make it read better. My only criterion for its publication is that a portion of any profits go to benefit the Traditional Hopi.

Kaih took on the task and completed the journey that brought White Bear's stories and the Hopi history to print.

Michael Lightweaver
Mountain Light Sanctuary
Asheville, North Carolina

www.mtnlightsanctuary.com

Part One

Custodians of the Ancient Way
White Bear and Naomi

Naomi and White Bear in the front room of their Sedona, Arizona home. Behind them are many museum quality art pieces made by the Hopi Nation.

White Bear and Kaih

Introduction

I met Oswald White Bear Fredericks through a Cherokee medicine woman. She had befriended me years before, when we met at Mt. Shasta, California. Clara was a master storyteller and many of her tales were about a remarkable Hopi man who lived in Sedona, Arizona.

I visited Sedona in 1988 where I received an invitation to meet White Bear at his home. He lived in a simple mobile home on White Bear Lane. Simple on the outside – but inside lived an art galley par excellence.

"Bear's" art pieces encompassed the walls surrounded by many museum-quality classics. Tables and bookshelves were covered with ancient sacred statuary, beautiful handmade baskets, ceremonial garments and moccasins from Hopi dances. Eagle and hawk feathers nested at the feet of White Bear's handcrafted kachina dolls. I was deeply impressed with their home – its beauty and balance.

At our first meeting, White Bear and his Caucasian wife, Naomi, were friendly but reserved. They gave me the opportunity to examine White Bear's creations – and their very impressive art collection. Then, they dismissed me as one might tell a child it was bedtime.

Over time, we met at restaurants in Sedona. They were amazing to watch. Regal to be sure, local celebrities, absolutely – totally enjoying the spotlight that followed them everywhere. They charmed everyone in sight! For example, White Bear loved chicken gravy and the waiter always brought him an extra bowl of it. But Naomi "Eats like a bird" as White Bear put it. Hearing his comment she would answer, "A vulture." To which their audience laughed until tears streaked their faces.

This was their public persona, but in their home (and in private), they were a very serious pair. During that time I was a journalist for *Challenge* magazine. White Bear and Naomi allowed me to interview them for a feature article in the periodical. Our friendship blossomed, and mutual trust brought an intimate relationship that we all enjoyed for many years. The magazine closed its doors in 1990, and White Bear and Naomi have passed on. But the memories of our times together live in my heart as a cherished treasure.

I have written a number of books that recount some of my experiences with these very wise and knowledgeable Elders. Due to my personal association with White Bear and Naomi, I was given the manuscript that has become this book.

The original manuscript was taken from a taped interview delivered by White Bear and typed by Naomi. The manuscript was completed in 1990 when White Bear was 85 years of age. It has been a rare privilege to be called upon to open for you the mysteries of history according to the Hopi perspective – at least according to One Hopi Elder.

My task has been to reformat and edit the material for clarity and grammar. However, I did not change the storyline or the information. I have no idea if the Hopi words are spelled correctly; I simply followed what was on Naomi's typewritten pages.

While working with the script I remembered the charming sing-song sound of White Bear's voice as he spoke. His first language was Hopi and he was quite eloquent in the English language. However, for readability I was required to change some of the sentence structure while also attempting to keep White Bear's style and charm.

I feel fortunate to have been a participant in this project and it is crystal clear to me that this is White Bear's book – about him and by him. It has been my privilege to make it readable; personalizing it with a few recollections of my times with him and the stories he told me over the years.

Many historians mourn the loss of chronological records from past ages due to the burning of the Library at Alexandria, Egypt.

The loss left a hole in the annals of time and in the truth of who we were in ancient ages and who we are capable of becoming today – and tomorrow. Thus, Atlantis and Lemuria are generally considered myths and theories – the true and real stories seemingly buried in antiquity.

White Bear's book brings us the chronicles of the *People who became the Atlanteans and the Lemurians*. This is human history at its most dramatic.

The color, the stories and legends – and the drama of White Bear's historical and illustrious verbal illustrations, demonstrate the romance and wonderment of Atlantis and Lemuria – and the tales of beings from outer space who personally interacted with early developing civilizations are fascinating.

This historical account of the emerging worlds of our past, also lays bare the truth that warring between nations can easily develop into violently unpleasant situations; creating circumstances that can cause the destruction of an entire world.

Today, we are in that moment when the Fourth World *must* become the Fifth World.

So how will we proceed? The choice is ours – we can destroy what we have – or if we decide on kindness and spirituality we can enter a higher consciousness – the gateway to a new Golden Age – alive in the Fifth World.

Who is White Bear?

He is a man among men ...

I purposely did not say, "Who *was* White Bear?" For he is still with us – through his teachings and the legends he shares. Because he recounted the history of the chosen people, and because he shares his life and its adventures, we are blessed to know the mysteries and the secrets of long ago. Yes, he has passed on but the legacy he left to future generations is priceless and alive.

White Bear *was* a full-blooded Hopi, born in Oraibi, which is considered the oldest continuously inhabited settlement in the United States. He was a member of the Coyote Clan and a nephew of Wilson Tawakwaptiwa, village chief of Oraibi. The blood of his ancestors is that of great seers and mystical people. Born with the knowledge of his forefathers he carried the sacred legends with him throughout his life.

White Bear was a prophet and historian, a singer, a painter and carver. Arizona considered him *the* Native American Artist of Arizona for many years. Senator Barry Goldwater collected White Bear's paintings and carved kachina dolls. It is said the collection, now languishes in a museum in Flagstaff, Arizona.

That is a bit of his résumé. Now, if I may, I would like to entertain you with my story of the man I knew as White Bear and his partner, Naomi. My knowledge comes from personal experience and from stories as they were told to me.

White Bear's story cannot be told without Naomi's companion story. They were more than husband and wife –

for they were destined to cooperate in a project unlike any encountered before.

Their love story

Naomi met White Bear on a golf course in Chicago. The fact that he was Hopi and she was Anglo (as she put it), never entered their minds. "We were two people who liked each other. It is the light and dark in our nature not the shades of our skin that counts."

"When I knew I loved him I had no idea of the adventure that was forming before me. We drove across country to his home on the Hopi Reservation. It seemed like any other long distance drive to me – that is until the lands of the Hopi People opened up before me."

"I felt it before I saw it! My God I felt *God!* My love affair was more than one man. My love affair was with lands that entered me and opened my bones – with a nation of people I had never met – with history and legend, ceremony and a way of life I could not have imagined only moments ago."

"I had become accustomed to the crowded high rise city of Chicago. I was happy there – but oh my God – when I saw the uninterrupted open high desert plains – the clutter in my heart disappeared and I knew this was my life, my destiny! This was my man – his people were my people – this was my land and I would do anything to prove myself."

She had to love it all in order to endure it. Naomi left a life she was comfortable in to enter a setting where even electric lights were unknown at that time. It wasn't an easy life on the reservation for a married couple of mixed bloods. Marrying outside the Hopi lineage was not a popular thing to do. "His mother was very sweet and encouraging. She understood ours was more than a marriage – it was a calling."

White Bear was *called* upon before he was born. Naomi told me, "While White Bear grew in his mother's womb it was not uncommon for high-ranking spiritual people to walk many miles to be in White Bear's mother's company – there to listen to the prophet (White Bear) speak – long before he was born."

As a boy he was *called* upon to help his father gather eagle chicks for ceremony – no job for a sissy. Mother eagles are not inclined to look kindly upon those who steal their chicks from the nest.

One of my favorite stories is about the first time the Master came to White Bear.

White Bear was visiting another Hopi village. It was late when he began his walk home – aided only by the light of a full moon. Lost in thought, he didn't notice the man walking beside him.

"Hello brother, may I walk with you?"

White Bear was surprised but not startled. "You can walk with me if you choose but we Hopi are used to walking long distances. I probably have about sixty miles to go before I get home."

They stopped for a moment. The man had a magnetic quality that drew White Bear's eyes to the man's face – whereupon the man looked tenderly at White Bear and said, "Oh my brother, I have come much further than sixty miles to be with you tonight."

When I asked White Bear to describe the man he said, "He was tall, much taller than me; his long hair was pulled back from his face. His eyes were piercing blue and moonlight seemed to gather around him causing his skin to glow."

"What was the man wearing?" I asked. White Bear simply answered, "A jaguar skin."

When I asked what the man's name was White Bear answered, "I only addressed him as Master – but you would know him as Christ – Jesus Christ."

Their first meeting was before the bombing of Pearl Harbor. At that time, the Master told White Bear about the coming of World War II and the atomic bomb.

At subsequent meetings the Master advised White Bear of his earthly mission. White Bear was to enter the world of the white man, for he was to become a bridge between modern society and the ancient civilization of the Hopi.

And so, White Bear left all he was familiar with to attend Haskell Institute in Lawrence, Kansas and Bacon College in Muskogee, Oklahoma.

In 1960, the Master informed White Bear and Naomi that they were to cooperate with others who would be sent by the Master for a project vital to human understanding and consciousness. And so a team formed to accomplish a Divine task. As Naomi said, "The lands at Hopi speak, inspire and conceive."

During a trip to Hopi country, Frederick H. Howell was deeply touched by the Hopi people and their history. He felt motivated to help create the *Book Of The Hopi* – (copyrighted in 1963, first printing 1969), through the

Charles Ulrick and Josephine Bay Foundation, the project was funded.

Frank Waters wrote the manuscript for the book from Naomi's typewritten scripts of recorded tapes produced on a wire recorder. White Bear and Naomi were the center of the project.

More than 30 Hopi spokespersons came to tell their clan's history – none received financial compensation for their efforts and contributions. White Bear said many of the elders who participated admitted they were sent by the Master.

When the interviews and tapes were completed, White Bear carefully transcribed the Hopi language into English – again, no job for a sissy!

Many Hopi words and phrases are not easily transcribed. But Charles Hughes of Columbia University had worked out a system for spelling Hopi words – and White Bear spoke both languages – and he had the help of the Master – and Naomi was there at his side doing the recording and the transcriptions, as well as typing the raw material.

There are many others who joined Creator's team who may not receive credit on this page – but the Master knows who they are and their reward is in His hand.

The Master told White Bear that the *Book Of The Hopi*, complete with White Bear's drawings and art (that tell a story all by themselves), would be invaluable to future generations of Hopi – primarily because the Elders who held to their traditions were dying and many young Hopi were entering the modern world. These young ones would not have the opportunity to listen to the legends and keep the history in the way that White Bear had. Also, the *Book of The Hopi* could be considered the Hopi Bible – a gift to *all* people.

To me, White Bear is a hero and Naomi is his heroine. They paid a dear price for the mission they accepted. He was considered a rebel, a renegade, a revolutionary – and unconventional among his people. White Bear and Naomi were hated by a large number of Hopi people for revealing Hopi secrets to the outer-world.

We are blessed to know a man of such character and courage – one, who did not flinch when his own people turned against him – a man who continued to value and love the very people who treated him with contempt.

Their home at Hopi was trashed and much of White Bear's art and Naomi's family treasures were destroyed. That is why they moved from their beloved Hopi Lands to Sedona – to be among people who respected and recognized their value.

When speaking of Native American Elders (with respect for their years and wisdom), we often call them Grandmother and Grandfather.

But in private, White Bear liked to be referred to as Papa Bear and Naomi told me to call her Mama Bear. This is how warm and personal our relationship became. Perhaps that is the reason this book project came to me. To edit and reformat, to be sure; but more than that, I have come to believe I was chosen because I could personalize this part of White Bear's book – to allow you to know the kind of people Mama and Papa Bear were and to tell you of their courage and strength – to tell you of their devotion to what they believed to be their mission.

In the chapters that follow my introductory pages, you will read White Bear's own words – the historian, the prophet – a man with a soul so artistic that the Master trusted him to tell the world the true history of Atlantis and Lemuria.

White Bear fulfilled his mission and his promise to the Master who guided his life's work.

White Bear – a man among men!

Part Two

As the Old Ones Told It

Grandmother Naomi listening to White Bear sing The Lord's Prayer in the Hopi language.

White Bear and Kaih

Preface

*This is the history of my ancestors and the clans
that came to this continent ...*

The continent of Lemuria where my people lived for a long
time was sinking under the ocean – the people had to leave
because of their conduct in certain matters. They migrated
to a new continent that was coming up from the ocean to
the east of them to make a new world – a new beginning.
You will read how my people came to this new continent
which we call the Fourth World, *Toowakachi*, and what
happened to them afterward.

First, I want to say that I am very, very grateful to the many
people who gave me knowledge and insight. Some of these
things were told to me as far back as my childhood. Some I
learned later when I was a young man and some I only
learned after I accumulated a good number of years. For
many, many years, great ceremonies have been performed
in which my people carry on the memories of our history.

We Hopi follow the maternal line in our families and
ancestry. Therefore I belong to the clan of my mother, the
Coyote Clan. I owe much of my knowledge to my mother
and grandmother – and to my uncle. They gave me
beautiful information.

My father's side (the Bear Clan), have been leaders and
chiefs of Oraibi for centuries and centuries. So what I
learned from my father and my uncle Chief Wilson
Tawaquaptewa, comes from their direct knowledge of the
history of the Bear Clan – and the other clans that settled
here.
There are also many others who shared with me their
wisdom and knowledge and to whom I am very grateful.

All of them belong to the clans that are now living in Oraibi. These clans kept their memories and their history alive – even through the hardships of their migrations. The migrations were carried out to fulfill our obligation to come to Oraibi (and establish a settlement), in fulfillment of the Creator's plans.

It is now the time for us to tell – to speak the truth about who we are and why we are here – hoping that some day, somebody will understand. Although I am the one who is speaking here, it is Hopi knowledge you are receiving. This knowledge is from the long, long history of my people. It is important that the whole world gets a warning. You will understand later, as we go along with my story, what I am trying to say. It concerns all of us. This is why I am speaking now. Maybe the warning does not come too late.

As I tell you our history, you must realize that time is not so significant. Nowadays, time seems important but time makes things complicated; time becomes an obstacle.

Time was not really important during the history of my people, nor is it to the Creator himself. What really counts is the beauty we bring into our lives, and the way we fulfill our responsibilities and obligations to our Creator. The material things of this world are secondary to the Hopi people, as you will notice when you are in my country and see for yourself the making of history as the Hopi live it.

When you are in our villages and among our people, you begin to realize that these old men and women who have created our realities today will never forget the old history they have written in their hearts. That history has been revealed to me and I will try to pass it on as faithfully as I can.

White Bear and Kaih

As you read the pages of this book, the old ones who inherited knowledge of the past are gone. There are few who still remember.

I am thankful that I sat alone, and received the knowledge of my ancestors.

The Early Times

According to our knowledge ...

We were in two other worlds before we came to the Third World, and then to the Fourth World which we are in now.

In the First World, man was created by the Divine Being, *Taiowa*. Taiowa, Supreme Being, created all things in the universe. There is nothing he has not made. He is in what is called "The Height" – many people call it heaven. Nobody knows where it is but it's from there that he controls this universe. He gave man intelligence to use – he gave his knowledge and all things man needed for his life. And he gave man the Law and the duties man has to perform in this universe.

The First World

The First World was destroyed by fire because so many people had become evil. But our people, those who were to become Hopi (in later times), survived the destruction because we were chosen to preserve the knowledge of it and to bring it into to our present world and beyond.

The Second World

The Second World was destroyed by ice. Again, our people survived and came to the Third World, the third continent. These, and later events still live in Hopi religious ceremonies today.

White Bear and Kaih

The Third World

The name of the Third World was *Kasskara*. Few people know the meaning of that ancient word now. I learned it from Otto Pentewa who remembered it. It means *Motherland* in English. We also called it *Land of the Sun* because we Hopi like to make references to the sun and the earth because they sustain our lives.

Kasskara was a continent – the same land that is now called Mu, or Lemuria. Most of the continent was south of the equator; only a small portion was north of it. It was a very beautiful land. Compared with the lands where we live today, it was almost a paradise. We had to work but we did not have to work hard.

From our beginnings in the First World, we followed the Creator's plan by planting our own food. At that early time, we chose corn as our main staple. We brought corn with us to the Second World, and we continued to use it in the Third World. We are still planting corn today. So, when you see our corn, you must remember that it has been with the Hopi for a very, very long time – ever since the First World.

[Editor's note: White Bear said corn is often referred to as Mother Corn because it is the only grain that produces milk when pierced.]

The knowledge we searched for and received was about plants and animals. We wanted to know what makes the leaves green and flowers colorful. We communicated with plants and animals. We had what you call scientific knowledge, but we did not use it to make things that are needed to conquer other people. People respected each other then. The clans had their own leaders but all were under one great spiritual person.

There is always one clan given authority for a certain period of Hopi life; to see that we carry out our duties and responsibilities – and to watch over our conduct. The Bow Clan had been given that authority when we inherited that part of the world. And so, the Bow Clan chief was the leader of Kasskara.

At the beginning (and for a long time), all was good in Kasskara. Much later (and gradually), people began to lose respect for each other – first a few and then more and many more. They took up responsibilities and powers without being ordained. You see – we are just like other people. I can compare that period to what we have in organizations today – people want rank and power, and they want to get their share. The same thing was going on in Kasskara. This was particularly so with the Bow Clan, but the top leaders of that clan remained good.

Now, before I can go on with the history of Kasskara, I must tell you that the Hopi were not alone on this earth. There were people who lived in other places.

White Bear and Kaih

White Bear and Kaih

Part Three

The Third World

Grandfather White Bear standing in front of one of his mystical paintings.

White Bear and Kaih

Atlantis

There was one continent to the east of us ...

And that is why we called it *The Land to the East –
Talawaitichqua.* In Hopi language, *tichqua* means *land* (the
surface of a continent), and the other part means *morning*
or *sunrise.* Between the continent to the east of Kasskara
was a long span of water. Nowadays, that continent is
called Atlantis and I will use that name because you are
more familiar with it.

At the beginning of the Third World, the people of Atlantis
were as peaceful as we. After all, we had both come from
the same Divine Source. They even had the same symbols
that we had.

But ... as time went on, the Atlanteans changed ... more
than we did.

They began to search into secrets of the Creator, secrets
man is not supposed to know.

You see, there are secrets that are reserved only for the
Divine Power. When mankind began to explore those
secrets, they violated that rule. Man has essentially the
same power as the Creator, but the Creator keeps secrets
for himself which man must not explore.

This thing with the secrets is very, very serious. So let's
talk about the time we live in now, to help you understand
what I want to say, so you find a basic idea of what the
Hopi believe. You have developed many things – airplanes
for instance.

When my uncle took me to the petroglyphs at Oraibi, which shows the jet plane and (of course), the petroglyphs are so much older than the jet planes of today, this is what he said to me, "It would be very nice to travel through the air like our people have done before. Suppose there is a catastrophe somewhere far away. We could pick up food and medicine and tools and help those people. But that instrument could also be used to destroy people hundreds of miles away. Then, they are violating the Divine Law."

How can you separate these two things – when you find secrets people are not yet ready to use in the right way? Think about yourself: suppose you have developed scientific knowledge in your field of rockets, and you let others learn it – and somebody else misuses your knowledge. Would that not be an evil use of the same knowledge? You would not misuse it, but *you* found that piece of knowledge.

Do you really know where your responsibility begins and ends?

Scientists are now trying to produce life, artificially, and to create humans one day. That belongs to what we call the *search into the blood*. And to do that is not good!

[Editor's note: Today's scientific cloning of sentient species rises from the experiments of Atlantis long ago.]

You can search into your body system to find out what makes you healthy and gives you a long life. That is what the Creator wants us to do. He wants us to enjoy this life here with as little hardship as possible, to get all the kindness and joy and happiness in this world.

We can sum up all in two sentences what The Divine Creator told the Hopi: "If you want to be my children, you must not use your knowledge to conquer, to destroy, to kill – you must not use my knowledge in any evil way. If you do so you shall not be My children."

Towards the end of the Third World

The top leader of Atlantis was a woman. In our language, we might call her *a kickmongwuity*, a chief priestess. In your terms, you might call her a queen. A very powerful and beautiful woman, she used her power and the beauty of her body to conquer the lesser leaders.

She got so much jewelry from her admirers that we call her Turquoise Woman.

Among the leaders who fell under her spell were high spiritual leaders. But let us say, they were questionable leaders because – a very spiritual man is not automatically a good man. She was very successful with these men and that is how she became the ruler of the whole continent of Atlantis.

Atlantis spread out its influence and conquered people in the lands that were farther east, those we would now call Europe and Africa. So, although Atlantis was not a big country, it had great influence. You may compare that with England when it was at its peak. That is a small country too, but what influence it once had!

Atlanteans searched into the secrets of the Creator – they were not given permission to do so. They were not prepared for spiritual knowledge and when they got it they used that knowledge to conquer others – thus they violated Divine Order. Some Atlanteans were so despondent they killed themselves following the violation.

The Atlanteans also explored other planets. They flew out to them but could not make their homes there because the planets they explored were dead planets. So they had to stay on this old earth.

Kasskara is Lemuria

There came a time when ...

The Atlanteans turned against Kasskara. They knew we were much stronger spiritually and morally and that made them envious. Their queen wanted to conquer our lands and make our people her subjects. She threatened our ruler, saying she would gather all her spaceships above our continent and destroy us from the skies.

[Editor's note: White Bear told me the weapon the Lemurians/Kasskarans feared the most was a sound machine more dangerous than many atomic bombs.]

The Kasskarans refused to obey the Atlantean queen. There was a long period of discussions and conferences. Meetings were held by all the great men of that time. Time and again, leaders came together attempting to work things out. But the group with strongly scientific minds dominated.

[Editor's note: White Bear's comment, "So reminiscent of today's world affairs."]

Some of the Kasskaran people got greedy for rank and power. There was a decline in our religious beliefs and there was very little respect among the people. We were in a situation which you can well compare to the situation now at this present moment in human history.

As time went on, the influence of the queen of Atlantis caused a division among our people. She began to win those who were power-hungry to her side. They moved secretly away from Kasskaran rules. "Maybe if I go with the Atlanteans and support their demands, perhaps I can get a good share later," they said. The evil force was getting the upper hand. These coalitions went into the Science of our Creator. Mankind was not supposed to enter into such knowledge.

The *good* people of Kasskara did not go along with that behavior. At that time we were known as the *Peaceful People* and we wanted to remain peaceful. Actually, I think it was the Creator who used His power to prevent us from doing harmful things.

What I am telling you now I learned from my grandmother. But I also talked with a man who was the last remaining authority on the Bow Clan. I wanted to speak with him because according to the story, the Bow Clan did the worst things. He confirmed to me what happened and said, "Yes, we did it."

There came a time when Atlantis attacked my people with their powerful inventions. This is what they did. From high up in the air they projected magnetic power down on our cities. Some of our people survived. Those who did not leave the true path of the Creator were called together in a certain area in order to be saved.

[Editor's note: White Bear's manuscript was written in 1990, so 'recently' might be in that time frame.]

Recently, at a village meeting in a Shongopovi Kiva, there was a long discussion about the situation the Hopi are facing today.

We see the same things happening now that happened between Atlantis and Kasskara – just before the destruction of the Third World. The reason why Hopi people are concerned is because we know what is going to happen. It became clear during that meeting that the main problem the Hopi are facing today is our land problem. It was also a land problem that brought the space people at the time of our Third World.

We know we humans have reached a point of no return.

[Editor's note: The point of no return is that moment when an airplane has exhausted the amount of gas that does not allow turning back. It is that point that forces the pilot to go forward regardless of what lies ahead.]

"We Hopi know humanity has reached the point of no return!"

The Destruction of the Third World

About Kasskara and the queen of Atlantis...

My people talk about the Third World and how it was destroyed. I remember my grandmother saying that what happened long ago between Atlantis and Kasskara could happen to us now.

The People of Peace used science only for good purposes. We searched into the secrets of nature. Our people looked for the power of the Creator in living things.

We did not defend ourselves when we were attacked. If that sounds strange to you, look at what Hopi are doing today. The U.S. Government *gave* us a reservation. Just think! How could they give us what was already ours? And from what they originally *gave* us, they came and cut pieces away making our "Reservation" smaller and smaller. Our land! But we do not defend ourselves with violence. Every time the government takes something away from us, we say, "That is wrong." Our Creator told us to say that.

In the time of Atlantis, although we did not actively defend ourselves, we had the shield.

I can tell you in your scientific language what the shield was, and how it worked. According to my grandmother, it worked like this: if you think of a bolt of lightening coming at you – it would get to the shield – then explode – but could not penetrate.

I remember clearly how she demonstrated to me the way the shield works. I was still a boy at the time. While we had our meal, she took an empty bowl, lifted it up and turned it upside-down and said: "You are here, under the bowl – if anything falls on it, it will never hurt you."

Maybe I should mention here that she had me repeat all the stories she told me over the years. Whenever I said something wrong, she stopped me and repeated what she had said before. This is why I know for sure all the things she told me.

Wars and Warriors

We knew we would not be destroyed – the destroyers always go first.

All the bombardment (or whatever it was), exploded "way out there" and the shield protected all the people who were to be saved – those that had been called together in a certain area. Only those in the safety of the shield were saved. The cities were attacked and people were killed there.

And then (as my grandmother said), somebody pushed the wrong button and *both* continents sank. It was not a big flood, the whole earth was not destroyed and not all people. Atlantis sank into the ocean very fast but the Third World (Lemuria/Kasskara) went down very slowly.

Let me explain to you why it happened that way. Suppose I intended to kill someone and I had an accomplice. We agree to do it. Even if I do the killing, he agreed, so he killed in thought. But he is not as guilty as I am. He will have another chance through reincarnation, but I will not.

Therefore, the sudden death of Atlantis came because they were planning the attack. Some of the Hopi worked together with the Atlanteans on their attack at Kasskara.

Therefore, there was less guilt on our side, and so our group was given another chance. If we had been as guilty as the Atlanteans, we would have been wiped out just as quickly as they were.

The Power, which is far beyond any human capability, would not allow the People of Peace to be completely destroyed. These people were reincarnations of others who had lived in that old Second World (*Tokpa – Dark Space)* and who had been abiding by Creator's Law.

That was the Creator's decision, and those that were to be saved were given the means to do so because we ARE the chosen people. We were saved because we have obeyed the law ever since the First World.

Next, we will see what role the Kachinas played in bringing us to this continent, the Fourth World. But first, I have to tell you a few things about the Kachinas.

About Kachinas

Since the First World ...

We Hopi have been in touch with Kachinas – *the highly respected Spiritual People.*

In earlier times, they were called *Kyapchina*, but since our language changes with time, we now say "Kachina." Actually, *Kyapchina* is the plural form. The word *chinakani* means a *sprout*, a new growth on a plant, and it is used here to indicate the growth in spirit the Kachinas give us. The full translation of the name therefore will be *highly respected Spiritual People of Growth.*

Kachinas can be visible and sometimes they are invisible. They come to us from outer space. They do not come from somewhere in our own group of planets, but from planets far away from us. It would take our astronauts generations to go there.

The Hopi name for these planets is *Toonaotakha*, which means they are closely linked together, not in a physical sense but spiritually; because the people "there" all have the same responsibility – they work closely together.

For that reason, I believe we can translate that word as *Confederation Planets.* And since we know that there are twelve such planets, we can also call them *Twelve Confederation Planets.*

The Kachinas can travel very fast. While I am speaking this sentence, they can go from here to there; it takes only seconds. Their ships go by magnetic force even when they fly around the earth.

Kachinas are ranked according to their accomplishments. All are called Kachinas, but some of them are also called *Wuyas*.

In the English language, *Wuyas* are called Deity. That is not totally correct because *Wuyas* refers to one who has a lot of wisdom, and can even be used for an old and wise man or woman. If you want to compare Kachinas and Wu-yas with your Christian ways, you would call the Kachinas Angels and the Deities Archangels. Both are Angels, but the higher ones you call Archangels. Or you might compare the Kachinas with working people and the Deities with a higher working class.

The Deities are over the Kachinas and above all of them is the Creator. Only Kachinas communicate with human beings. The Deities do not – they give directives to the Kachinas.

In our society, all children (all of them), are first called Kachinas. That is done to get the child used to the Spiritual People. It would be hard to explain such things to them. That is where the kachina dolls come in. The dolls help a child become familiar with the appearances of the Kachinas so they will not be scared when they see the kachina dancers. Outsiders who buy Kachina dolls don't know anything about them so they are inclined to call everything a kachina.

We do the same thing with the San Francisco Mountains. They are visible and they are high; and so, a child can understand that the Kachinas go there when they leave us. It's similar to what your people tell your children about Santa Claus and Christ Child.

But when the child is initiated, that is when he is told the truth. To the mature mind, a Kachina is from a far away planet and when he leaves us he goes back there. And the men (here on earth), who are doing the dances (representing Kachinas), are portraying Spiritual Beings of various ranks that come to us from other planets.

There are three kinds of Kachinas. The first has to do with the continuity of life. In our ceremonies they appear in the middle of the winter, when all life in nature is dormant. They assure us that life will continue. And because reincarnation is a part of the continuity of life that means that we can be reincarnated; that we will have another chance to improve ourselves.

The second group of Kachinas are the teachers. From them we learn who and where we are, where we came from, what is influencing us and what we should do.

The third group are the Custodians of the Law. They can also be called the Correctors. They warn us to make corrections in the way we live. But there comes a time when they no longer try to correct; they then punish us for the evil we have done.

There were children born as a result of some mystical contact between Kachinas and our women and I will tell you legends about that. Our people could touch Kachinas, so there was physical contact between human beings and them.

But as strange as it may sound, there never was any intercourse; there was no sexual contact. The children were conceived in a mystical way. Such children, when they grew up, had great knowledge and wisdom and sometimes supernatural powers, which were given them by their Spiritual Fathers who were wonderful and powerful men – always ready to help, but never to destroy.

The Kachinas are physical beings and this is why they need flying vehicles for their travels in our air and for traveling back to their home planets. These vehicles come in a variety of different sizes.

We have various names for these flying vehicles. One we call *Paatoowata – Water Shields* (the object that can fly through water). *Pahu* in my language means water, and *toowata* means an object with a curved surface. We also call them *Flying Shields* because of their shape.

I will explain what a Flying Shield looks like. If you slice open a gourd, you get a shape that looks like a bowl or a saucer. And when you put two such pieces together, you get the shape that the Kachinas used at that time for traveling to the planets. If you sit in an object like this, the thing can go back and forth and you will not fall off, no matter how fast you go. That is the reason for the shape and that is why we also call it *Inirsa* or *Held in a Bowl*.

Because this object looks almost like a gourd, we also call it *Tawuya*. It is common knowledge among the Hopi that some of our people traveled in such ships.

We know that such vehicles were also used in other countries because the Atlanteans came over to us to attack us with them. Near Oraibi, we have a petroglyph that shows a woman in a Flying Shield. An arrow indicates that it flies with great speed. The woman has the hairdo of a married woman.

There is a thong that ties the two halves of the flying ship together. All the man who flies the ship has to do is to use that thong. When the thong is twisted to the right the ship goes up, and when he twists it the other way it goes down. The vehicle does not have an engine like our airplanes; it has no fuel. It uses the magnetic field. But you have to know your altitude. If you want to go east, you go up to a certain height, if you want to go north, you go to another height. All you have to do is fly up and then the ship goes in whatever direction that altitude relates to. In this way they can fly anywhere inside our atmosphere and they can also leave the earth.

It's that easy!

Migration to the Fourth World

We will now continue with the historical event ...

Long before the sinking of the continents of Lemuria and Atlantis, the Kachinas discovered that a part of the world was rising above the water to the east of us. I may add here that our knowledge tells us that the world has changed several times. So what was coming up then was actually the same land on which we had lived in the Second World, *Tokpa*; but we call it now the Fourth World because it has a new surface.

[Editor's note: We know the Hopi People dwell in Oraibi and the Mesas at Hopi Land which White Bear describes as the Fourth World. The Fourth World began in colonies that started in South America and then migrated to continental North America. Tokpa, the Second World and the Fourth World can be considered the Americas.]

According to the Hopi People, the earth has flipped over a few times. I mean that the north pole was then where the south pole is now, and so on. Right now the poles are reversed. The real north pole is at the south pole, and the south pole is at the north pole. But in the Fifth World (the one to come), that will be corrected and the poles will then be in their proper places. Such flip-overs were always completely north to south. They never were halfway, because that would have destroyed too much and that was not the Creator's plan. One such flip-over occurred in Tokpa, the Second World, and it froze everything.

The Kachinas were watching and investigating the new land. When the land was above the waters they prepared for us to come. Then the great migration began. The new land would be the place for us to settle and it would be called our Fourth World, *Toowaquachi*. We also had another name for it: *Sistaloakha*. That word means anything that happens fast and appears in completeness.

So, the Creator decided that he would save us – the Kachinas helped us come to the *new* continent.

[Editors note: Let us recall, Kasskara (Lemuria), was slowly sinking. And the people were facing imminent danger.]

There were three ways by which our people came from the Third to the Fourth World. According to our people, the first method was by Flying Shield. That was for the most important people, those of the highest order. They were the privileged ones because they had to establish the new settlement (in this new world), and to prepare its function. Because they would be arriving first, they were naturally considered to be good people. The Kachinas (being space people), knew where the new land was and brought the good people there. Only the Kachinas could do that because they had the Flying Shields but our people did not. We could not build them. Do you remember that the Atlanteans did have Flying Shields? They did not get them from the Kachinas who left them behind – unfortunately, they learned to build them with their evil power.

The first clans came to the Fourth World long before the whole continent of the Third World had sunk underneath the ocean. The names of some of the clans that came by Flying Shield are: Bear Clan, Fire Clan, Snake Clan, Spider Clan, Bow Clan, Lizard Clan, Eagle Clan and Water Clan.

Actually, there were more clans transported by Flying Shields but I give you only the more important names here. In the whole list, the Bow Clan is much farther to the end than it looks here, because they had done that evil thing in the Third World, but Bow Clan people were still important. Although many of them had been involved in the destruction of the Third World, not all of them left the true path of the Creator, and so they were saved.

There was another way by which people were brought to the new continent. That was by means of powerful birds. That is still remembered in the initiation ceremony of Powanu in March. I myself have gone through this ceremony at Oraibi when I was initiated into the Powanu Society.

Before the feathered hoop initiation the chief sings to us about the world we had left. His song tells us of the wicked queen who conquered most of the world, and how badly she corrupted it.

During the ceremony, each child who is being initiated steps into a wooden hoop. Feathers are tied to that hoop all around. These are the feathers of the strong birds: eagle, hawk, owl and crow. Only the strongest feathers of a wing are used. Twins, a boy and a girl who are ordained for that purpose, move that ring up and down along the body of the initiate four times. And that reminds us that this is how part of our people came to this continent, on the back of strong birds, particularly the eagle.

The group that came to the new continent on the backs of these strong birds were those people who were in the transition of understanding the higher goals of spiritual knowledge. At that time, people were very afraid because the continent continued to sink under the water.

Even though we knew that we would be saved before the whole continent disappeared it was frightening to see city after city destroyed. The water seemed to multiply from

itself and covered more and more of the sinking continent –
the Third World.

The last of the groups to leave the sinking continent were
those who were just beginning to search for the knowledge
of spiritual power.

My clan, the Coyote Clan, belonged to that last group,
according to the knowledge of my mother and her parents,
who belonged to the Coyote Clan. They knew that
definitely because it had been very important that these
events were remembered and passed on as a gift to *this*
continent, the Fourth World.

The last group of people used a third method to come to the
new continent. They traveled by boat. They really had to
struggle hard and for a long time. So, while in fact, many
people were flown over to the Fourth World, people are
still told today that everybody had to struggle hard to come
to this continent. We do this so that we don't forget. Why?
Because if you earn something the hard way you will
respect it more and protect its memory.

All the people who traveled in boats were of minor clans
with little power. And because they were minor clans they
easily fell under the influence of the Bow Clan; some
participated in the Bow Clan's destructive plans in the
Third World. They went along – but did not initiate things
on their own. Therefore they were not as guilty of the evil
part as the Bow Clan. For that reason, they were given a
chance to escape the destruction of the Third World.
Otherwise, they would have been wiped out.

The group traveling by boat was brought safely to the new
continent by the Kachina People. Each clan had a Kachina
whose duty it was to come with them and guide them. So,
even though the last group came by boat, they were safely

conducted. The Kachinas communicated with them, but the people in the boats were not privileged to talk with the Kachinas.

The people (in their boats), went from island to island in a generally north-easterly direction. The Kachinas gave them advice on how to protect themselves, and also directed them so they could find the islands. On each island, the groups rested before they continued their journey. Finally, the people in boats arrived in the Fourth World.

The voyage by boat is remembered in a ceremony performed by the Flute Clan. It takes place at a specially built, round well a few miles west of Oraibi. The name of that well is *Muyio Watki*.

At some point during that ceremony, the priest stands in the middle of the pool facing east, because that was the main direction of the boat people's travel. He is up to his waist in the water. Around the well, people are standing who sing about the migration. The priest has a woven paddle in each hand and makes paddling motions when water is mentioned. That means he is in a boat. When land is mentioned in the song he crosses his arms over his chest and puts the paddles under his arms. That indicates that he is resting, and his people with him. When water is mentioned in the song again, he starts paddling again. This is the way the memory of our migration from island to island, from one stepping stone to the next, is remembered and kept alive.

That same event is also remembered, or you might say documented, by the group of seven figures on Easter Island. They look in the direction of our migration, and there are seven of them as a reminder of the seven worlds we have to go through. Easter Island is the only one of these islands to which we came that did not sink completely under the ocean when our migration was finished.

By flying space ships, on the backs of eagles and by boat – these were the three ways in which all groups were brought to the new continent to establish their settlements. They established their colonies on the continent that lies south of the United States – now called South America. The highest part of that continent had been above the water for many years.

Not all people who survived Kasskara (Lemuria), came to the Fourth World. We, the Coyote Clan, were the last of the chosen people who left the sinking continent. Those that were rescued after we left were taken by the currents to other places. Some of them landed on Hawaii which was a part of the Third World that was not submerged. Others came to the South Pacific Islands, and there were even some that went to what belongs to Japan now.

I learned this only a few years ago. At that time, I was visited by a young man from the Hawaiian Islands. He read the *Book Of The Hopi* and told me that his grandmother had told him exactly the same stories about the ancient worlds as in the *Book Of The Hopi*.

There were a large number of people who did not come to South America – even though they were of the same stock as the Hopi, and came from the same continent, Kasskara. This is why, for instance, in Hawaii the Spiritual People are called *Kahuna*, which is the same word as *Kachina*.

The Fate of the Atlanteans

Not all the people of Atlantis perished
when that continent sank ...

Many Atlanteans were saved who did not agree with their queen when she attacked Kasskara. Naturally, when the Atlantean continent submerged the survivors wanted to come to our new continent. But the Creator promised us that this new land would be solely ours for a long time to come.

The Creator did not want the Atlanteans on the new continent. He sent his Kachinas to prevent the Atlanteans from moving westward. Although these survivors never wanted to go along with their spiritual leaders – they still were Atlanteans.

In earlier times, when the Third World was established, the Atlanteans did have Kachinas. But the Kachinas left when the Atlanteans became evil.

So now the Atlanteans could only go east into areas which we now call Europe and Africa. Their power had been taken away from them; they were earthbound and could no longer fly. The only way for them to survive was to go in independent smaller groups – some here, some there. And each of these groups carried with them only a piece of the full knowledge they once had.

This is why the Atlanteans of today have no recollection compared with the Hopi knowledge of true history. When they destroyed the Third World, the Creator placed their culture on the low end of things.

White Bear and Kaih

The Atlanteans were punished for many centuries. Then they began to develop, to come up – to evolve.

People around the world think of Egypt as ancient – that is only recent, as we Hopi see it.

This is our people's knowledge.

Part Four

The Fourth World

Grandfather White Bear making Kachina dolls.

The Fourth World – Toowakachi

Toowakachi ...

Continental America is now the Fourth World, *Toowakachi*. That word means *The Land Beautifully Established for all People*. It is our knowledge that the Hopi came here first, and that the Creator promised us we would live here alone – for a long time.

We are at the center – the middle of the Fourth World and the life span of the earth – and of mankind.

We are in the fourth of seven worlds that mankind is to experience. Now we have three behind us and there will be three more to come. This knowledge is expressed in the deep-set rituals my fathers (the chiefs), have performed. Hopi knowledge is also expressed in the many ruins that have been found in Mexico and South America – and North America as well. As far as time is concerned we are already past the midpoint of the seven worlds because their length gets shorter with each new world.

[Editor's note: According to White Bear, there are Nine Worlds that humanity will experience. The first seven pertain to our evolutionary endurance. The eighth and ninth are beyond endurance, evolution, egos, needs, training, education and willfulness.

Interestingly, mystics of the East speak of seven chakras related to the human form, an eighth just above the head and the ninth connecting us to the many universes. The human form is more than a body – it is the most complex machinery imagined. Humanity has continued to look "outside" seeking "who we are" when actually "here we are" intact broadcasting and receiving stations of a most unique design, and with a most unique purpose. Each one of us is a "World," one we have continued to destroy and migrate from, always aiming for a better place and time. The 'Worlds' White Bear speaks of can be physical realities of constantly elevating states of Mind.]

The part of the new continent that rose above the water first is called *Taotooma* – this is an abbreviation. We often make such abbreviations in our language. In English, that name means, *where the arm of the sun touched*. In this case, we do not say, *taowa-tookoni-ma* which means *sun-arm-touch*, we make it shorter and say Taotooma. But it means: *the place where the arm of the sun (that is the beam of light), touched the earth*. That area was the first to rise up above the ocean.

According to the Hopi People this was the new land the eagles sighted. They were sent out from Kasskara while it was sinking. They flew up very high and while gliding on their wings they saw our new land. That is one reason why we have to respect the eagle.

The time came when we were on the new land. Eventually, the last group arrived, after migrating by boat from island to island.

With their arrival the migration was completed. And as we stood on the shores of the new continent, we looked back and saw that all the islands were sinking beneath the sea. The Kachinas gave us the Third Eye and we saw it all – the Motherland disappearing and the islands too.

[Editor's note: Except for Easter Island which remained as evidence that the People of Peace had been there long ago.]

Not all of the people that came to the Fourth World and lived in Taotooma were Hopi. Our ancestors were among other people. Of the many who came to South America, only those who eventually came to Oraibi were called Hopi; and they were called Hopi only after they were accepted in Oraibi.

Age passed into age, from the time the first people (those that came by Flying Shields), arrived on Taotooma, some of our people say it was about 3,000 years before our people were *all together* again – but it was actually a thousand years more. So this first period was about 4,000 years long. Actually, the *beginning* of the migration (the arrival of the first clans by Flying Shields), was about 8,000 years before this present time.

In our language we have a simple way to talk about long time periods. We say: one *Soomody* is one thousand years. *Soo* means star- and you know there are many stars are in the sky. So we use the number of stars for the number of years. 4000 years are therefore only four *Soomodys*. That was the time it took to get all of our people together again. It was eight Soomodys ago that the migration began.

Those who came to the Fourth World could come only to this one location for Taotooma was not big.

My people know that they were the first ones on this continent, and the only ones. There were other tribes here in America but they came long afterward – after the ice in the north had melted.

A very long time (before the migration), our Creator had shown us the planets. After he molded us into the living beings that we are, he offered us great opportunities.

But we failed. We went away from the direction he gave us. We went away from his Law. And this is why this piece of earth, this small piece of land (that many refer to as

Hopi Land), was to be our part of the world – the place where we had to learn again to control ourselves and how to live with one another.

Titicaca

When the first people landed ...

They did not go directly to the place where the first city was built. According to our story, when the first people were looking for vegetation and water they saw big footprints. They were puzzled because they thought they were the first. They followed the footprints for a while and then they saw *Messao*.

He was sitting at the base of a rock with his chin in his hands. He welcomed them and told them he was the custodian of this land and that he had been waiting for them for years. He said they were on the *atvila* of this land, meaning its western slope.

Our people told Messao that they had done many wrong things and they did not want to corrupt the lands again. They asked him to be their leader. He answered that he would not but they were still welcome to live there. He let them know that he would be coming to them if they did wrong again.

So they built their first city on the new continent.

The first city on Taotooma was *not* built at the top of the mountain but below it. And it was built by the people who came to the new continent in Flying Shields. They were privileged to use these vehicles because they had to provide for the new settlement and cause it to function for all the people who would come later. Today this city is called *Titicaca*.

I will tell you how it came about. The city of Titicaca was a big city – bigger than any city we had in Kasskara. It spread out almost like the city of Los Angeles today. The center of the city was where the lake is now. There in the center of the city, people worked and lived. You know the ruins of Tiahuamacu which are not far from the lake? Tiahuamacu was actually part of the city; outskirts you might say.

Taotooma was not big compared to all the people who came. The land was not yet prepared for cultivation because it had come up from the sea. But the Creator ruled that everything had to be provided for us. And since the Kachinas were still with us, they showed us how to plant food in the early morning and *harvest the crop by sundown*. That was most important over a period of many years – until the water began to recede.

The population grew bigger and bigger and bigger. The water continued to get lower, and more land and more islands appeared. Our people began to move north, south, east and west. We began to investigate that growing continent by means of Flying Shields. Some of our people were of such a high order – they were so close to the Kachinas that they could fly with them from one place to another – to see where future settlements could be built.

And then, slowly and over a long period of time, there were again people who had different ideas about obedience to the Divine Creator. They began to sway away from the true path the elders had known. In that group there were highly ordained people who wanted to go to other planets and be leaders there. They began to misuse the Tawuya. And they were the first of our people who ever misused them. We had never done that before.

The Kachinas tried to convince our rebellious ones not to attempt to go into space. The Kachinas said, "Space is to be left alone until you have taken care of your responsibilities in the present world." But this group of people thought they were ready for it.

The Creator knew what was going on and it did not take very long for him to come down. At that time he said to us, "You have already failed your first opportunity on this new land. I have to punish you."

He took our city, lifted it up, turned it upside-down, and sank it into the ground. That part of the city is now at the bottom of the lake and that is why nobody has found it. All the rest of the buildings (around the area), felt the force of the extreme air movement caused by that event – and they felt the vibrations in the ground: it was like an earthquake.

Our Creator was disappointed that we had disobeyed him again. At the first opportunity! And because of our indiscretion, our people decided that they must move away from there.

The people spread out in different directions. The first dispersion of our people on this continent had begun.

New Migrations

About another 4,000 years ...

That's what it took for all our people to arrive in the Fourth World – I remember, my grandmother gave me this information around 1914.

The whole continent on which we were living had risen above the water (in the form it is now), and the land became usable.

Our people gradually moved away from the ruins of Titicaca, the first city built in the Fourth World – particularly those people who still lived in obedience to the Creator. They wanted to separate from the others in order to maintain their true faith and to continue their mission. Because of that many settlements were built all over South America.

Our people did not leave all at once. Their departure was spread out over a long period of time. Again Kachinas were assigned to each group to guide them. The groups (we call them clans), had to move away from each other in order to survive and to stay with the teaching of our Creator – which was part of the Divine wish.

The Kachinas communicated among themselves. During this migration they helped us in much the same way they did before. They showed us again how to harvest food *in one day* – and not have to wait for months for harvest.

During that migration we got farther and farther apart from each other. We were soon many miles apart but the Kachinas, because of their knowledge, created communication between the clans. During that time they also taught us (or tried to teach us), to come back to obedience to the beautiful Law that was given us in the beginning.

During the migration from the first ruined city, the Kachinas provided information to certain boys and girls *who were not born yet*. These children were destined to carry on the true memory of what happened in the past. This has continued throughout our history. While the child is still in the womb of its mother, the knowledge is given to him. Even before that, the mother is sometimes given this knowledge, so that her thoughts can penetrate the child's mind before his or her birth. Therefore, the child does not have to learn later, she or he need only to be reminded of the knowledge they received before they were born.

Many centuries have passed since the beginning of the migration we are speaking of. But the teaching of the Kachinas kept our knowledge alive. The Kachina People often went back to the Creator (with the speed of lightning), to tell him what progress we were making on earth. Also, during this time (as I mentioned earlier), some of our people were so high and so close to the Kachinas that they could fly with them on their flights over the land.

To repeat, the waters had subsided and the land was dry enough so we could continue our migrations. It was very difficult for us, but the Kachinas guided us to areas where we could live for awhile. They did so even though we had been disobedient. Why? Because children were born and would be born in the future. It is for their sake that the Kachinas continually remind us of the past.

Bear Clan Migrations

*My story has the clans migrating and
moving in different directions ...*

Now I will continue by telling you the history of one clan.
That will be the Bear Clan, the clan of my fathers. They
were the chosen leaders for the Fourth World.

I received most of my knowledge from my father and his
brother. They had a thorough knowledge of the history of
where we had been and how we came to this hemisphere.
My ancestors have been the leaders of the Bear Clan and
the Hopi people since our arrival in the Fourth World.

Before I go on, however, I will tell you something I know
from my mother's mother. When we left the big ruined
city, the Spiritual People wiped away the memories of what
had happened. The minds of those that stayed there were
cleansed for all future generations. In this way, no one
living near the ruins (later), would have any knowledge of
what had happened. Of those who were left, only the Hopi
would know.

In the Third World, the Bear Clan had been one of the less
important clans. They had not participated in the
destruction of any of the previous worlds, which says they
had not been a powerful clan. Because they had no evil
record they were chosen to be leaders after they arrived in
the Fourth World. So now the Bear Clan ranks higher than
the Fire Clan that destroyed the First World – or the Spider
Clan which destroyed the Second – or the Bow Clan which
destroyed the Third World.

Because of the Bear Clan's high position as leaders of the
Hopi People, a Kachina of the highest order was assigned

to them. In fact, it was not a Kachina but a Deity. His name was Eototo. He was assigned to them wherever they would go.

As the Bear Clan went northward in South America (following Eototo's directive), they experienced great difficulties. The area through which they were to migrate was terribly hot! They had come from high elevations to the lower valleys with dense forests. It took them a long time to get through those forests. Their breath was short, their children died from the heat when they were born. These were very hard times! The climate was so hot!

Our people wanted to find mountains where they could get fresh cool air and be away from that oppressive heat. The Kachinas encouraged them to continue their struggle. The Kachinas investigated far beyond the lowland where the people were and so directed the people safely.

A number of clans left the great ruined city after our clan. And they went in different directions. Such groups, including the Bear Clan, already knew what was ahead of them because the Kachinas working with the various clans were in communication with one another by mental telepathy. In that respect there was no distance between them. Distance did not count if they wanted to talk to one another – and to see each other. Therefore, the Spiritual People could see what progress the groups were making on their way through the jungle.

The people were in that hot climate for a long, long time. Finally, they were released from the heat and jungle vegetation. The people began to breathe much easier, and children no longer died from the crushing heat and humidity. They kept on migrating northward, and they found lakes and rivers because they were directed by their Deity, Eototo.

Our people began to increase in number. Many years went by. The migration brought them to an area that had a wall of ice. They could not go farther north. That location is not far north from where the Canadian border is now.

Eototo told them this was a door that would be opened later for others who would come and migrate south. Eototo said, "Now turn around and find healthier areas to live."

But their journey was not yet ended. First they had to migrate towards the *rising sun*, through areas that the water had drained off not too long before. They then came to a place where they could not go on because ahead of them was a great sea. Their Deity told them that this was *Paasso*, the end of the eastward journey. That was of course important to them. *Paahu* means *water* and *soota* means *the end.*

"Now," the Deity said, "You must turn around and walk in the opposite direction towards the *setting sun*." They followed his orders and went west. It took many years until they came again to an area where water was before them. Again their Deity told them that this was *Paasso*.

In reverence, the Hopi put their heads against the incoming waves and let the ocean wash their hair. This was done to purify them so they would not be destroyed by water again. They did that in the east and they did that in the west.
Then Eototo said to them, "You have now completed your migration, now you can choose where you want to be."

But the clan was not really sure where they wanted to settle. They made journeys (here and there), to many places. After they had seen many lands, they established their permanent village in Hopi Land. The Hopi have lived in these lands ever since.

Palatquapi

The trouble in South America ...

Long before the Bear Clan established Oraibi (while other clans were still wandering in South and Central America), some of the clans wanted to be reunited.

They remembered the trouble in South America (at the time of the destruction of their first city), and wanted to live together again – to live together again *in harmony* with the Great Spirit, Taiowa.

They had disobeyed him and were now split up and scattered in all directions. Influenced by their Kachinas they were determined to come back to the true path. Those leaders who could still use their Third Eye brought their clans together to establish a cultural center of the highest spiritual level.

A Third Eye exists on the top of our head when we are born. It is the soft spot which closes in twenty days after birth. Until the soft spot is closed the child communicates (through the Third Eye), with the Creator.

[Editor's note: In some cultures the Third Eye is said to be in the center of the forehead just above the eyebrows and related to the pineal gland. However, White Bear told me the Hopi believe the Third Eye is at the top and center of the head. And that it is a real eye that could be compared to a radar instrument that continually tracks the Will of the Creator. This Eye is located in what some cultures describe as the Crown Chakra. White Bear said the Eye is asleep in most people and that as they educate themselves in spiritual matters the Eye opens and can see beyond human realities.]

Some of the people of this age can use their Third Eye – all their life. There is no limitation for them. All knowledge can be acquired – how this life began and what happens hereafter. They can see the creation of life and they can see life on the other side. Naturally, they can see the things that exist in their time and they can look into them. In the terminology of our present time I can perhaps best compare it with x-rays, although in certain ways the Third Eye is more powerful.

Going back to the cultural center devoted to the highest spiritual level and the city it languished in – this area is remembered by every Hopi clan. I don't believe that any single Hopi could ever forget Palatquapi, the city. In our language *Palatquapi* means *Red City*. According to my grandmother, Palatquapi was the first big city in the central region of the western hemisphere,

During that same time, the groups who did not come to this great cultural center, declined further. They began worshiping the sun as their god and continued to do so.

The Bear Clan came through that area long before others, as they moved on toward North America to claim Red City for the Hopi.

The place where the Red City was built has been found again. It is now called Palenque and it is located in the State of Chiapa in Mexico. It was a large community in the past. Contrary to rumors it was not built by slave labor. Building it was no hardship. The basis for all their work was spiritual.

Whatever people contributed to that community was done for spiritual reasons. These people had come from a great disaster that happened to their first city and they wanted to prove to themselves saying, "We can do much better now!" They wanted to cleanse themselves.

Those of High Order came together creating a great renewal of communication – contact with the Space People (the Kachinas), was renewed.

The Great School of Learning

The levels of learning ...

In Palatquapi, the people built a learning center with meticulous devotion. This was the most important building in Palatquapi for it was to be used for learning. My father told me about it when I was a youngster, before I went to school. He said that the learning center was one building consisting of four stories. They were used in the following way:

On the ground floor, young people learned the history of their clans and of the previous worlds. More or less, what they were taught all the time. The upper levels were the essential ones. Let me tell you more about them.

On the second floor, the people learned about the life plan. They learned everything about nature. In their studies they learned about plants and animals by actually seeing them grow. They saw how flowers are produced – how insects, birds, other animals and all living things under the sun come about. They saw how such things mature – and how they develop into the forms they have. Here, students were also encouraged to open their Third Eye and taught how to use it.

Students also learned about the chemical substances which make up our life. The body is composed of the elements from the soil. So when we do not obey the laws that affect our soil we suffer physically – and spiritually.

The diseases that haunt mans bodies have come to us through man. This comes about through those who are the evil people we call Two Hearts today.

White Bear and Kaih

Such evil continues from world to world – and it still goes on today! And evil will continue until the Creator himself eliminates it. But that will only be in the Ninth World.

Along with learning, students on the second level also produced the food for their community. So the people were eating food of the purest possible nature plus adding spiritual nourishment for the body.

This taught them great respect for all things that surrounded them. They learned it was in accordance with the order established by the Creator that they could use plants and animals (and other things), to maintain their bodies and also to make their homes.

But first, a prayer had to be given to acknowledge (as a gift), what they took for their use. In this way they do not destroy, they are receiving gifts; and the life around them will be the same in the future as it was when they received it. Even today, any Hopi who has spiritual understanding will acknowledge and offer his thanks. This is very important and our people should continue to do it. So, the second level was the real beginning of learning about life and these students carried such knowledge throughout their lives.

On the third level of the learning center were men who had gone through the studies of the other levels. On the first two levels students were between about twelve and twenty years old. By the time they graduated to the third level, they had been in contact with different people, various minds and ideas. They were old enough now to observe, and to experience more. Now it was time to learn about the human body and mind and our connection with the Divine Source.

First, third level students were taught about the head. The Creator has given us this beautiful instrument for knowledge – the brain. The brain is where our thinking and our ideas work together with all the other physical parts of a human being.

These students also learn the structure of the mind, and how the Creator works with mankind – and all living things in the universe. When a person thoroughly understands this, there are no language barriers. You can communicate with all plants, you can communicate with all animals – you can communicate with any species in this whole world. What they learned on the third level was how to get this beautiful mind tuned to work with God (as you call him), or the Creator according to our people.

Second, they learned about the importance of the voice. The vibrations of our sounds are not limited only to the people who listen, they reach the whole universe. And therefore the sounds that come from us should be harmonious. When we speak harmoniously we are praising our Creator. For this reason the Hopi (in his ceremonies), through his songs praise all the nature around us – and all the elements. This is done in devotion to the great power of the Divine Being.

All things we say are continuously recorded – and yet, all one speaks in a lifetime takes less than a small pin head to store it. You see how backward, how antiquated your tape recorders are? All voices, everything that was ever said in the Third World, is stored in a cave in South America. My grandmother told me about that once. She also said that nobody knows where that cave is now.

Next, third level students were given the teachings about the heart. In the heart is the truth of what we think of other people for our heart is the seat of compassion. In the heart we find understanding, which is so important.

Another important aspect of our heart is its connection with the blood which sustains our physical life. And because blood is so significant, man must not experiment with it. The Creator forbids the misuse of blood. We were told great danger from the misuse of blood would come in the future.

Now we come to the top level of the learning center. On the top floor students learn about the universe around us, about creation and Divine Power. They learn about every aspect of our planetary system. Not just what one can see but also what is invisible.

They learn also about cosmology. These students knew then and we know now, that modern day astronauts would find sand on the moon, that the earth is round – that there is no life on Venus, no life on Mars or Jupiter. These are all dead planets, not for man to live there. If your scientists had asked us, we could have told them that they would find sand on the moon.

[Editor's note: White Bear told me that he was brought to Earth from Mars accompanied by a Kachina. White Bear gave me the distinct impression that he had lived on Mars. Perhaps he was brought to Earth because Mars was in the process of dying. Only conjecture on my part.]

Top level students learned the Creator has a universal plan and that man has to follow that pattern. When man violates Creator's pattern he is no longer the Divine Power's child and will be punished. *The Creator's requirements sound very simple but they are hard to follow.*

Anything that brings harm to a human being, anything that is contrary to the peace of mankind is against the Law. It follows that the worst crime somebody can commit is to take the life of a human being. There is nothing that can be worse than that.

Next we learned about the Eighth World. That world exists now although nobody knows where it is. All the people who die go there. Actually, that world has two planets, one for good people and one for evil ones.

When the Eighth World comes to an end, all the good people from the Seventh and the Eighth World will come into the Ninth World. So the Ninth does not yet exist but will be established in that future time, right here on our earth. This Ninth World will have no end, it will be infinite.

Evil people will then stay forever on their planet, blind and in darkness.

[Editor's note: We see now why the *Book Of The Hopi* is referred to as the Hopi Bible. The correlations of characters and references to good and evil, heaven and hell are all present. Both books are ancient, legendary and historical in their nature.]

In the Ninth World there will be no race differences. You may have to change to my skin, or I into yours, we don't know. But there will be no different races. There will be work to do and everything will be wonderful. But there will be no such stuff like you Christians say – angels and all those people playing on the harp; our Creator is not a lazy person.

I remember so much about the teaching and learning. The learning center's building, with its structure and levels from the ground to the top floor, illustrated to our people a

White Bear and Kaih

continuous increase in knowledge, the ascending to higher spiritual levels and accelerated understanding of the wonders of our world.

According to my people, a structure like this was also built in the city of Titicaca.

The teachings at the learning center were done by the Kachinas. The Creator knew about our progress because of his communication with them by mental telepathy. The decision as to who would go to this School of Knowledge was made by the Kachinas, because they are the ones who preordain the children before they are born to this life of learning, devotion and sacrifice.

Only Kachinas know. But no man can judge who is to graduate from one level to the next, and eventually, who can reach the last step in this great school of understanding.

Some men fail early and will not come to the next higher level, and others may fail later. Only a few people attain the highest goal. Their physical and spiritual life is in harmony with the Divine Creator; and therefore I will call them *the great Holy Ones.*

One of the Great Seers

His Name was Aapa ...

I must tell you about a man who I have been fortunate to know. He belonged to the clan of my grandfather, the Badger Clan, and was one of the great seers of our time.

Such seers are sometimes called medicine men (even by our people), but that is not what they really are. The experiences I had with Aapa and what I witnessed through him were truly great mysteries to me.

He often used his Third Eye. Once he told us that he can go from this side (the physical existence), to the other side – the spiritual world. According to him the partition between these two existences is thinner than anything in this world. Anyone who can use his Third Eye can penetrate it.

Aapa also demonstrated to us how we could look to the other side of the earth by using the moon. He showed and taught us many things you cannot believe unless you see them yourself. He did such things in the presence of my mother and father – and being the oldest son I was also allowed to witness them. I could tell you more about him but it would be too hard to understand and almost unbelievable for anyone who has not had such experiences.

Aapa told us that it was from that fourth level of the learning center that such knowledge had come to the people, and that he received his knowledge from his ancestors.

People like Aapa, who devote all their time to such important tasks, walk a very narrow path. It is a path exposed to many dangers and the temptations that can come to a man are immense. There have always been some men who attain such high goals. Today the name for such a man is *Nakela*. This word means *encourager* or *counsel*. Such a title indicates sacrifice and limitation of his daily life – for his duties as a teacher to his people. Such a man must not let anything come into his mind that could lead him away from the path of the truth.

To those who reach this high objective, the Kachinas extend the privilege of not having to die. Such unselfishness allows them to leave this earth without having to face death. This happened once in the city of Titicaca. A group of high teachers actually went off in their physical body and traveled to a planetary system that is not known to us.

The Kachinas encourage us to learn and to go on to the highest ordination possible. They keep reminding us that our life is before us – and how much we can achieve if we will preserve what was learned in that great center and school of learning.

They told us that at some time in the future there would be trouble again. And they told us what we must do to continue in the presence of Divine Power.

Decay and Trouble

Some of the clans began to move out ...

The people of Palatquapi traveled on the right path for centuries. Everything was harmonious. Gradually, as time went on, some of our clans began to move out. The more new settlements spread out the less communication we had with our teachers, the Kachinas.

Men who had reached the highest level in our great school were sent out as emissaries to the various communities that developed. These men used their Third Eye to find among the young people those to whom they would pass on their knowledge.

Eventually though, many settlements lost contact with the teachers who were guiding us. That set us on the wrong course. Differences began to develop within and among clans. Such discrepancies caused clans to split, and more people moved away from Palatquapi. They went into Central America and the Yucatan. They built cities there and also on the islands off the Yucatan coast. These were great civilizations too.

Then the point was reached again when even spiritual leaders went over to the evil people – even our spiritual leaders strayed from the true path. The time was coming when there would be another disruption of our people.

The most important clans that moved away from Palatquapi were the Snake Clan and the Bow Clan. However, parts of these clans remained in the city – those who were still abiding by the laws of the Creator. I'd like to tell you about the structure of our clans so you will understand how such separation worked.

Compare a situation with two brothers. Both have the same family name. So, if one of them moves out you would have part of that family in the city and part of the family somewhere else.

Let me show you how that works with our clans. Let us take the example of the Snake Clan.

Like other clans the Snake Clan consists of several groups. In this case there are six such groups, which are also called clans, because we have a six-directional snake. The highest group is the Kaatooya Clan. *Kaatooya* is the snake to the west (the direction of sundown, of death), and is the highest ranking snake. According to the Snake Clan tradition, Kaatooya passes judgment on you when you pass from this earth. Kaatooya is of course the highest Deity of the Snake Clan but we speak of him like he is a snake.

The Ancient Sky People

A most unusual ceremony ...

I will now describe to you a ceremony that reminds us of our time in the jungle. It demonstrates how the Hopi people needed guidance so they would know where to go and to be protected from wild animals. I have personally witnessed this ceremony. It is performed every four to eight years at the time of *Shaatlako (the Tall Kachinas)*. The ceremony is very unusual because there is no dance – they just march.

[Editor's note: In this script, when you see Kachina spelled with a capital 'K' that is to indicate those who come from the stars as teachers and guides for the Hopi Clans. When you see kachina spelled with a small 'k' that is to indicate a human dressed in ceremonial garments and regalia representing the role of Kachinas in Hopi history.]

In this ceremony a group of people march along accompanied by four kachinas: one is leading them, one is behind them, and there is one on either side of the group.

Before I explain to you what that means I will describe the two most important kachinas: the one in front and the one behind the group. The dancers represent very high-ranking Kachinas (Deities), and they are called *Solawuchim. Soo* means stars (as I have told you before), *la* means continue, or contain, and *wuchi* means they have been ordained. The meaning of their name can therefore be translated as *the large stars that hold the secret knowledge.*

Both representatives of the Solawuchim have an archer's bow in their left hand and a quiver made of jaguar skin over their shoulder. This is to show their strength and power.

White Bear and Kaih

A black line is drawn across each face which hides the eyes. This distinguishes them as holding the secret knowledge of their homeland. Large black and white neck pieces indicate their knowledge of the heavenly bodies. The blue color of their moccasins means that they are Spiritual People from far beyond the stars. One other important thing, both wear a woven type of legging, called *Ruokenapna*, which signifies they represent Kachinas of a high rank.

In their right hand, both hold an instrument made of the hip bones of small animals. The dancers make a clanking noise by shaking the instrument up and down. One wears the skin of a jaguar indicating he is the leader. The dancer representing the Deity with the *horn* on the right side of his head follows the group from behind. He is the second in command. The blue diamond pattern on that *horn* represents the electric or magnetic energy which connects his home planets.

The kachinas that walk alongside the group are of a lower rank. They have only bow and arrows and carry a long stick, but they do not have the instrument that produces the clanking noises. It is very important that those representing Deities and Kachinas belong to the Bow Clan; because it shows that the Bow Clan had the same experience as the Bear Clan.

I am now going to tell you what the ceremony of the Tall Kachinas represents. Qoch-hongva, or *White Clouds over the Horizon*, of the Sun Clan first told me the story many years ago.

His knowledge came from his father. A year later I learned the Solawuchim belonged to the Bow Clan: Qoch-hongva did not tell me that. So I contacted Tewaletsiwa, or *Sun Standing Up*, of the Bow Clan at Old Oraibi, who was the last of his clan to have this knowledge. The story he told me mentions the same basic events and also agrees with the Bear Clan memories I have spoken of earlier. The Bow Clan, the Bear Clan, the Sun Clan and the Coyote Clan have the same knowledge in this respect. The difference is that the Bow Clan story is the most complete of all and that is only natural because the Ancient Sky People dance is performed only by the Bow Clan.

Now the story: the Bow Clan began its migration (to the north), into the jungle region; from a city they call the Fog City because fog often came over the city. The Hopi word for that city is *Pamisky*. It was located high up in a mountainous area – but Tewaletsiwa said he did not know where in South America that city was located. "If I would see it, I could easily recognize the place where Fog City is located. Tewaletsiwa also knew about Taotooma.

The Kachinas told the Bow Clan that they would have to go into the jungle. The clan left Fog City and went down to the lower altitudes. I gather Fog City was somewhere in Ecuador.

When the Bow Clan was ready to go on its migration, the Kachinas came to help them through the jungle. They showed the clan where to go and they protected the people on their march. The protection was necessary for the sake of the children. None of the children who migrated from the highland survived. Only those who were born in the lowland survived.

When the clan rested during the night the Kachinas became like stars that rise above the jungle and with their light they protect the people from animals. During daytime the Kachinas guided and protected the people in the manner which is illustrated by the ceremony. The Deities made the clanking noise with their instruments and the other

Kachinas hit the ground with their sticks. This was done in order to frighten away the wild animals. It is only now that bones of animals are used in our Hopi ceremony to produce the sound. The bones are substituted for sea shells which were used at that time of the migration into the low lands.

[Editor's note: We read that the migrations of the People of Peace were often challenged by oceans and seas. The presence of sea shells would remind them of their journeys. But when the Hopi ceremonies were held in the high desert the bones of small animals were substituted.]

According to Tewaletsiwa the shell instruments also sent out magnetic waves. He was serious in telling me about the vibrations and noise of these shells.

Today, buckskin is used at our ceremonies rather than a jaguar skin. The ceremony is important because it gives the Hopi people knowledge of the struggle they have lived through.

I might also mention that the bows of the Kachinas were only for protection. The Hopi people did not need to kill animals to survive. In Taotooma the Kachinas had urged the people to live less on the meat of animals but rather on vegetation because that would make it easier for them to maintain high spiritual knowledge. The Kachinas stayed with the Bow Clan until they arrived at Palatquapi.

There is a snake and a clan for every one of the five directions. Some of these Snake Clans disobeyed their Deity *Kaatooya* in Palatquapi and went away. But three clans – west, east and north remained with their Deity. Therefore we can say at one point that the Snake Clan left the city, and at another point that the clan was in the city. Do you see how there is no contradiction? In this particular case, those of the Snake Clan who moved away made war later against their own highest Deity.

As I have said, the clans that moved away from Palatquapi built many cities. The ruins of some of them have now been found but more will be discovered in the future – and with them more evidence of the accuracy of Hopi knowledge.

The major city of the Bow Clan was the great center of Tikal. A stone sculpture of a head with a snake in its mouth was found there. That is the Deity *Saavki.*

Yucatan was mostly settled by the very powerful Snake Clan. They also built many cities and you will find the plumed serpent on many rocks there. Their main city was Chichen Itza.

The leaders of these clans moved away from Palatquapi because they wanted to assume authority of their own. Soon they began to feel they were just as powerful as those of Palatquapi. They left the true path and went their own ways.

Up to this time and early in this phase of splitting and moving, Palatquapi was the true center. We called the new cities on Yucatan and in Central America subsidiary cities. But when clans moved away from Palatquapi, power was taken away from Palatquapi and its leaders anticipated war. Many clans held on to the truth. Most of them remained in Palatquapi – but some were among the clans that left. These clans could hold on to the truth because way back in the early times they did not take part in the destruction of previous worlds. They were the *chosen people.*

The highly ordained people (those who had reached the goal of the fourth level in the learning center), saw the danger of impending war. And so, they went out to the cities and attempted to reunite them. But they could not control the clans.

There were many wars in that general area. The Snake Clan and the Bow Clan had many battles with each other. These wars eventually led to the complete downfall of all cities.
The whole area became so corrupt and disrupted by the violations of Divine Law that the people did not want to live there any longer.

Everything was affected. They could no longer carry on or perform their religious duties in the true and correct spiritual way. Therefore the only thing they could do was to leave their cities and migrate once again. And so, they left their cities behind, and some of these clans after a long time eventually settled in Hopi Land at Shongopovi and later in Oraibi and then in Hotevilla. That is why the Plumed Serpent ceremony is still performed in Hotevilla every February.

It was during the great troubles in Palatquapi and in Yucatan that the Kachinas left us. They have not been with us since that time and we can only imitate them in our ceremonies now. As they left they told us: "From now on you are on your own."

[Editor's note: Yucatan is a state in the country of Mexico, located on the Yucatan Peninsula.]

You may have wondered why there could be so much trouble in Yucatan and Palatquapi while the Kachinas were with us.

When war and violence take place it is not the Kachinas who plan them, it is man. The Kachinas warned the people but most wanted to conquer others – to make war. *They did not listen then and they do not listen now.* Mankind continues to violate the Creator's Law.

Many clans and people have been exterminated. Whenever the clans made war, the Kachinas kept their hands off. They did not want to get involved: *"This is man's earth, it is his responsibility and he can follow his own ideas."*

When man willfully harms another he does it on his own. Man will be punished but the time for punishment has not come.

There are several legends about battles that took place in that long ago period of unrest and decay.

I will tell you two of them: the story of Hahai-i Wuhti, and the story of the battle between the Bow Clan and the Snake Clan. The story I will tell you about Hahai-i Wuhti happened during the final attempt to capture Palatquapi. The Bow Clan battle was one of many that were fought in Yucatan.

Hahai-i Wuhti

A group of clans migrated north ...

Disagreement among the leaders developed when they reached the ice barrier. Some clans followed the true knowledge but others deviated. The clans who strayed decided not to continue their migrations but to return to Palatquapi.

The clans returning from the north developed their own ideas and teachings. When they eventually got back to Palatquapi they saw a prosperous city and noticed that the people were still following the beautiful old teachings.

The wayward became envious. The people of Palatquapi and the newcomers could not live together because of their different beliefs. And so the newcomers built their own settlement not far from the city. They were of a very powerful clan – the Fire Clan. This was the clan that had authority in the First World and had caused its destruction.

The envy and jealousy of the Fire Clan people eventually made them attack Palatquapi. Our memory of this battle is kept alive in some of our ceremonies in which the heroes of that battle participate.

One of the clans that stayed in Palatquapi and had not continued their migration was the Assa Clan. In my language, *Assa* is the mustard seed, which was part of our food during the winters in the early days of our stay in Oraibi. The name of that clan changed later to Astak Clan, but at that time it was still Assa Clan. The people of that clan were obedient to their leaders and faithful to the teachings of the Spiritual People.

Among the Assa was a family with three children, a girl and her two brothers. They came to play important roles in one of the great events in our tribal history. The name of the girl was *Hahai-i Wuhti*. She was quite obstinate and hardly obeyed her parents. The characteristics in that girl brought about the downfall of Palatquapi and that era. But she was strong and although she was the youngest she was not afraid to do a man's work when her brothers were not around. The oldest brother was *Chackmaina*, and the other brother's name was *Hooto*.

Palatquapi had a stone wall all around the city therefore was well-protected. It had been attacked many times but each time the city fought back and destroyed the enemy.

When the Fire Clan began its attack, it was Hooto the younger brother who ran to the house of his family to tell his parents.

At that moment the mother was combing Hahai-i Wuhti's hair. She had just completed the squash blossom on her left side and was combing the hair on the right side.

[Editor's note: The squash blossom (or butterfly) hairdo is worn by Hopi girls following a four day puberty ceremony. The hairdo signifies the girl is now a young woman ready for marriage.]

A few moments later Chackmaina (the elder brother), rushed in and also told them of the attack. He then looked at his sister who was sitting in front of their mother, and he said, "You have always been a headstrong person. You have not obeyed our parents and did not follow what our mother told you. Now let's see how brave you really are and if you can help defend our city." "I will show you," Hahai-i Wuhti said to her brother.

Before her mother could tie the squash blossom on her right side of her head she got up, went over to the dwelling's wall, picked up a bow and arrows, and ran out.

She did show great courage during the battle and it was her oldest brother who caused her to do it. Everyone fought bravely. Chackmaina was in the midst of the battle, facing many enemies, when he was shot from behind. In his pain he cried out, "Hu-o!"

In our ceremony, the dancer representing Hahai-i Wuhti carries a quiver, bow, and arrows, and half of her hair is hanging loose. The dancer portraying Chackmaina cries out a loud "Hu-o," the very sound shouted during that long ago battle is repeated in our present-day ceremony

Hahai-i Wuhti led her people in the big battle. They drove the enemy out from the city and so far away that the city was never attacked again. Hahai-i Wuhti, Chackmaina, and Hooto became Kachinas because of their heroic actions, and they appear as featured dancers now in several Hopi ceremonies.

During the dances the dancers who represent Chackmaina and his sister do not walk gently and orderly. They act violently, reminding us of their fights during the defense of the city. And Chackmaina's loud "Hu-o" is a repeat of his outcry when he was shot.

In our ceremony, Hahai-i Wuhti leads the kachinas into the village singing the song of her actions during the battle. She carries a quiver on her back, a bow and arrows in her hands, like she did at the time of the real battle. She carries a rattle like when she was running out to fight. This gave courage to the warriors. And so, before the dance begins she shakes her rattle.

Being of strong character and great courage, Hahai-i Wuhti and Chackmaina do not have to be in line with the other dancing kachinas. They can break away and dance outside the formation. Hahai-i Wuhti is the prominent figure in the dance and none of the other kachina dancers can ever get ahead of her – they must always stay behind her to demonstrate the leading part she plays.

During this ceremony, their masks are black. That has nothing to do with race but it shows that Hahai-i Wuhti and Chackmaina have become Spiritual People, no longer human beings. Because of his black face, Chackmaina is now sometimes called *Spirit of the Night* but that is not a full explanation. In its true meaning black is the symbol of anything mysterious, those things only the Creator has knowledge of.

During the ceremony, on one side of their faces they have a moon painted, and on the other side a star. These two symbols are very significant.

The moon, as we know, is far away from the earth but she is still visible. The moon indicates a great distance in space. That leads us to recognize the greater distance of a star than that of the moon. The star indicates the planetary system in which the Kachinas live – the Kachina's home star. The home star's planets are not known to the astronomers of today. That planetary system will be known only towards the end of the Seventh World. At that time we will learn of the Confederation of Planets. But our current knowledge and science cannot penetrate into that region.

Hahai-i Wuhti has another symbol on the back of her head. It shows a green field and two black markings on a blue background. The blue represents the blue of the sky you see when you look up and is therefore a reminder of space. The inner areas and markings are an indication of the planet she comes from.

So you see, we have great commemorations of the actions of Hahai-i Wuhti and her brothers in our ceremonies. It shows you that we maintain the memory of our history and that we have the true knowledge of what has happened.

The Snake Clan and the Bow Clan

This is another important story ...

Time had long passed since the battle of Hahai-i Wuhti took place. Our people migrated many miles before we came to our present home. But the knowledge of these true events has been kept alive. The members of one particular clan (who are still among the Hopi people), do not like it. I will relate the story because it is well-supported by evidence in the form of the petroglyphs and sculptures that have been found.

Like I said before, a division developed among Hopi spiritual leaders. Some wanted to continue teaching the young people according to the Hopi's great spiritual heritage. The Snake Clan was one of these faithful groups. But others like the Bow Clan did not want to continue in that way. The Bow Clan acted like this when that clan participated in agreements leading to the destruction of the Third World. This is common knowledge among the Hopi people.

We know about the powerful weapons that were used in that battle. *Such knowledge is again being developed scientifically in many countries in our present world.*

The Bow Clan claimed their way of life made them more powerful, and so they challenged the Snake Clan. Other clans also accepted the challenge.

Before I go on with the legend I must tell you a little bit more about the Snake Clan. We Hopi are the only ones who have the symbol of the six-directional snake. There is a snake to the east, one to the north, to the west and to the south. But in addition there is one in an upward and one in a downward direction. These are the spiritual directions which were guiding the various Snake Clans at that time.

Every one of the six snakes has a special meaning and responsibility. I will not describe them all here but will only talk about the clan that was of importance in this particular battle. The snake that points downward works below the surface of the earth. There is a desert snake that actually buries itself in the sand. We call it the Sand Snake but it is better known under the name *Twuachua*, or *Sidewinder*. Because of the power of that snake, the Snake Clan was asked to defend the city – and you will soon see why.

The leaders of both sides came together to determine the rules of the battle. These were big arguments – like they have today among the leaders of the nations. It was agreed the battle should begin two days after the end of the meeting. Each side was determined to conquer the other's city within four days. The Bow Clan wanted the Snake Clan to begin but the Snake Clan said: "No, you have challenged us, therefore you begin."

The Bow Clan would be the first to attack. The battle was to begin every day at sunrise and was to stop when the sun touched the horizon.

Now this war was not to be fought in the usual way with clubs, bows and arrows. It was not a war of man-to-man fights. This was to be a scientific and technological battle between two very powerful groups whose cities were about 50 or 60 miles apart. The Bow Clan and the Snake Clan do not like to speak about this event – even today.

Preparations were made for battle during the following two days. When the sun came up above the horizon on the third day the battle began. The Bow Clan bombarded the city of the Snake Clan with the most powerful, vicious weapons they had. What they used was what we now call electric power; it was something like a bolt of lightning.

The Snake Clan was prepared for that. The snake I mentioned earlier helped the clan so they could be below the ground and were protected by a firm shield – and also powered by electric power.

While still under the protection of the shield, the leaders of the Snake Clan briefly came up above ground to see where the sun was. Sunset came as a great relief. Sure enough, at sunset all became quiet. The sound of thunder occurred every time that terrific force hit the Snake Clans' shield. But now all was quiet. The shield was put away and everybody came out into the open. The Bow Clan people knew they did not damage the Snake Clan – and that tomorrow it would be the Snake Clans turn to attack them.

Now the Bow Clan had to prepare its defense

The new day arrived and the Snake Clan attacked the Bow Clan's city which was many miles away. So powerful were the weapons of the Snake Clan it was almost like shooting atomic warheads, But the Bow Clan had its shield too. You see, both groups were far advanced in their knowledge.

They survived that day, and the battle continued with no decision on the third day. With that the Bow Clan lost its chance for victory. The fourth day came – the last chance for the Snake Clan.

The Snake Clan did everything in their power but they could not penetrate the shield of the Bow Clan. After many hours the Snake Clan decided that they would have to do something more extreme to show their power. So, sometime in the afternoon the Snake Clan stopped shooting. Then, according to the Snake Clan, they put to work the power of the snake that can bury itself. They made a tunnel that went underneath the defenses of the Bow Clan.

The Bow Clan people were puzzled when the bombardment stopped before sunset. They wondered why the battle had stopped. What had happened? They thought the Snake Clan had given up. But while the Bow Clan people were in discussion, the Snake Clan leader came out from the tunnel and shouted to them: "I am here! You are conquered! We could have killed you! We will not kill you. But from now on your Deity *Saaviki* must carry a snake in his mouth every fourth year at our ceremony."

That was the end of the battle. There are petroglyphs in our lands showing a man with a snake in his mouth, and there are sculptures showing the same in other places, Tikal for instance. And this is the reason why a snake is carried in the mouth of the Bow Clan Deity during the *Powanuya* ceremony here at Oraibi. This will always remind the Hopi people of what happened in Yucatan long ago.

Dispersal

After that very troubled time in Yucatan we broke apart. Palatquapi itself was not destroyed by the wars. But people moved out and the city lost its power, and eventually it was destroyed by an earthquake. Many clans began to migrate again, sadly isolated from each other.

The Kachinas helped only by giving us directions. No longer were any spacecraft used on our behalf. This time we really had to struggle. Now we had to earn this land in order to call it our own. The migrations must go in all four directions. The people came from the south so they still had to go north, east and west.

Our people migrated all over the North American continent. Ruins and mounds all over this continent are witness to our migrations.

We were the only people who built permanent homes during the migrations. The Creator wanted us to do that. We were not just putting up tepees or light huts but built solid houses in which we would sometimes stay for years before we would move on. Such settlements, or ruins, will indicate to other groups who come later, that we were there; and that we were there a long time before them.

There were groups who disobeyed. Some began their migrations but did not complete them; others would just stay put as soon as they found an area they liked. Only a few clans maintained faithful and obedient to the laws and the true knowledge. Others lost devotion to the religion of our people and they lacked our true knowledge, although they too were created by Taiowa.

Casas Grande

The clans were spread out far and wide over South and Central America – and into North America. The few clans that still carried with them obedience to the true law began to look around for spiritual leadership. They wanted teachers because they knew they could not depend on themselves for guidance. They had respect for the teachings of the past and their teachers and believed the teachers could bring the people into harmony again.

A few of the spiritual leaders decided to bring their clans together once more. They wanted to teach the younger generation – and advance them to the highest order – that place of understanding that the human relationship with the Creator is Divine. The spiritual leaders wanted to pass on to the young ones the beautiful knowledge that had been preserved since the First World. Through all our wanderings and all our troubles, our devotion to Creator's Law has never been forgotten.

In that era, the wonderful city of Casas Grande was built. There seemed to have been only four important clans gathered together in Casas Grande. Today, we find the symbols of the Eagle Clan, the Snake Clan, the Corn and the Ghost Clan in the ruins. Destroyed structures are there which may have symbols of still other clans.

I remember clearly when I sat with my father one day – at a time when I was still going to school. He asked me what we had learned – I think he was not satisfied with what I told him because he began to tell me about the Casas Grande settlement. I was fortunate to visit it many years after that day. I found it just as it had been described by my father, and it was the way his brother described it to me at a later time.

My father and my uncles had never been to Casas Grande. How could they have known its history – its secrets? It is because they were told the history so many times by their elders. That is the way we preserve our knowledge.

Four clans and their leaders worked hard to get other clans to come and learn at Casas Grande and for some time the city was a great center.

The end of Casas Grande came when the Spider Clan attacked it. The clans that lived in the city defended it bravely. But when the enemy cut off the river which brought water into the city, they had to give up their defense. They did not surrender but dug a tunnel through which all the people escaped. The Kachinas didn't go with them. But they made the people invisible so they could get out without being seen by the enemy. This city was the last big gathering place of our people before the final meeting at Oraibi.

Oraibi

"It is known that the true knowledge will come from here."

Oraibi is the oldest village on this continent. It has been continuously inhabited since it was first established. Even scientists have to agree with that statement (to some degree at least).

Scientists checked trees which had been used in building our homes and they say that the village was established about 1150 AD. That may be old in terms of your history but *not in ours*. That is only a few centuries, and after all, what they examined was only the oldest piece of wood they could find. *There are three earlier villages underneath the present buildings.* Oraibi was actually founded about 4,000 years ago.

[Editor's note: The *Book Of The Hopi* describes Oraibi as a village clinging to a 600 foot high escarpment rising abruptly out of the desert plain.]

In the Hopi language the word *ora* means rock, and *abvi* indicates a high place. Oraibi means therefore a *rock place up high* and that is correct because there is a big rock up there at the edge of town right next to the village. In the early days it was called *Ojaibi* but since our language changes (as I have told you), it is now called *Oraibi*.

White Bear and Kaih

But Oraibi was not the first place ever built in this area. The name of the very first village was Shungopavi and it was built below the present village of the same name at the foot of the cliff at Second Mesa.

After the people lived there for awhile, trouble developed between two brothers. The trouble involved the wife of one of the men. The younger of the two (his name was *Machito*), decided to move out of Shungopavi, where the brothers had lived. Machito went on to establish his own village. He called it Oraibi and it is still Oraibi today.

Being of the Bear Clan, Machito (having all the knowledge of his ancestors), brought along with him some of the most important things the Hopi possess; *the four sacred tablets*. These tablets were given to him by his elders when he decided to build his own settlement.

[Editor's Note: There are many and varied stories attached to the current status of the Hopi sacred tablets. It is said the Bear Clan tablets spoke to the traditional settlement pattern of the various clans. The tablets also determine the boundaries of Hopi lands and recognition of the symbolic authority of the Bear Clan.]

Machito was of the Bear Clan. All the leaders that came after him were of the same clan, even up to our time. Machito's name comes from his habit of putting corn kernels between his fingers. We call that machito and that was how he got his name.

It took hundreds of years for all the clans to arrive that were called to come to Oraibi. The clans designated to settle there were chosen long before Oraibi was even established. And even these clans could not come when they wished to. Their Kachinas were there to guide them, to say, "Now is the time for you to go." And then they went – and they came. That was also the last time the people were allowed to *see* their Kachinas, to see those great Deities. From then on other Kachinas were assigned to be with the clans, but in spirit, not in physical form, *remember that.*

All the clans that came to Oraibi were required to settle a few miles away. There are numerous ruins in our area (which at some point in time), were such settlements. After awhile the settlers sent their leaders to our chiefs to ask for permission to settle permanently. To be permitted, they must tell their whole history; the story of their migrations, where they had been, what they had done, and if they had obeyed the laws. All their history had to be revealed to my fathers – the Bear Clan.

But the completion of the migrations was not enough to be admitted to Oraibi. The clan leaders must also tell what their function would be in the sequence of our ceremonies throughout the year. There is a full cycle of ceremonies, completed only when all individual clan ceremonies are present and fit together. So, a clan that wants to move into Oraibi must be able to contribute their own ceremony to our full cycle.

The first clans that came here after the Bear Clan were the Ghost Clan, the Spider Clan and the Snake Clan. The clans that participated in the ceremonial cycle were selected because those clans were living in accordance with the Divine plan. That is a narrow path that only a few can walk.

Some clans were not admitted – they were of the same Hopi stock but they had not completed their migrations. They settled in our general area and are now called the Pueblo tribes. I might add here that *pueblo* is a Spanish word. As far as we are concerned we always call them by their real names.

Like for instance the *Si'os* which are now mostly called *Zunis*, or the *Lagunas*, the *Pawaatees*, the *Hootitn*, and others.

There were also clans that were not accepted for other reasons; the Assa Clan for instance. They lived in Chaco Canyon for a while and they wanted to join us at Oraibi. They performed their ceremony but our chief said no, "We cannot use that." So they remembered the lush green fields somewhere in the south and began to migrate there. A long time later they became the great *Astak* nation. I told you that the Assa Clan was also called Astak Clan at a certain time. The Spaniards made *Aztec* out of Astak.

As I said it took hundreds of years before the clans were all together. My clan, the Coyote Clan, was the last to come to Oraibi.

We were always the last. It was so at the time of the great migration from Kasskara (Lemuria), to this continent, and it was so in Oraibi.

This is not because we are slow but is to be interpreted as "our fate." It is like a signal: when the Coyote Clan comes – that is it! No other clans will be accepted. For that reason we are also called the *Door Shutters*. This is also the reason why kachina dancers wear a fox tail on their backs. When we moved from Sikyatki to Oraibi, after the big race we were again the last. No one came to Oraibi after the Coyote Clan arrived.

Oraibi is located in a very arid region and it is not easy to see why we settled there for good. Let me tell you the reason. The Bear Clan did not come to this area by chance. They were told to do so by their Kachinas' Deity because it is near the Center of the Universe. This Center is actually located in the lowlands about two miles south of Oraibi.

That area is called *Tuwanassawi*. Those of the Kachina Clan settled there once. Today you can still see a ruin there.

Today our great village is rumbling because we have reached the end of a period. We will rebuild Oraibi in the Fifth World but that will naturally be in a different location. Maybe our present Oraibi will be rebuilt as a national monument one of these days. One thing is important to remember, so I will repeat it: only after a clan was allowed to settle in Oraibi permanently were its people called Hopi. Those that clung to the laws of the Creator, *the chosen ones,* the very few, came here and became Hopi.

While we were still migrating we were called the *Awl People* which is *Mooch I* in our language. You can see again how the Spaniards mispronounced our names when they called us the *Moquis*. Our people were always a small number, compared to the large number of tribes throughout thousands and thousands of years. There were always tests and trials and failures to weed out those who did not comply with Creator's Laws.

Even in Oraibi we had our problems, and even in this time span. There was a disagreement that developed among our people not too long ago – just as it did long, long ago in Palatquapi. We disagreed and we repeated that split at Palatquapi. People moved away from Oraibi and established Hotevilla and then Bakavi – or they moved to Moenkopi and Earthmoving. See how history repeats itself?

Huck'ovi

I have heard this story many times – since my early childhood. *Huck'ovi, Windy City,* was built on the next mesa just across the lowlands from Oraibi. The memory of that event is kept alive because it tells us what can happen to the whole world today. We will realize when the time is near, because we will see the same things taking place.

The village was established by the Forehead Clan. This clan is one of three clans that are connected to heat and energy. It is heat that destroys and it is also heat that purifies. That is why these clans are so important. In the order of their power these clans are: the Fire Clan, the Sun Clan and the Forehead Clan. Their highest deity is *Machaqua*, the *Horned Toad*. This is why we find the horned toad etched several times among the petroglyphs down on the cliffs. The Fire Clan people are well-known for what they did to the First World: they destroyed it.

The Forehead Clan got its name during the migration. Of these three clans they were the last to arrive at the Atlantic Ocean; the Fire Clan and the Sun Clan arrived much earlier. So the Forehead Clan had to hurry and they could only rest their forehead on the beach for one night and then they had to hurry on again. That's why they are called Forehead Clan. And because they were late and had to hurry, they have less authority and less power than the other two clans.

There came the time when people in the village failed to follow their chief. It got really bad – there was disobedience and the people stopped responding to the chief. By an old rule the only way to correct this situation was to abandon and destroy the village. This happened before in the Third World, with the cities of Titicaca, Palatquapi and Casas Grande.

History keeps repeating itself. And it is being repeated worldwide today. Just think of all the disobedience nowadays – and the lack of respect. This is why we Hopi know that the end of the Fourth World is coming fast. We are right on course – again.

So back to my story – the decision was made and the people agreed that the village would be destroyed. This was to take place after a last ceremony – to be done by explosion and fire. Some people remained in the village for they did not believe fire and explosions would happen. All the others left before the ceremony.

The ceremony was performed by thirty women and thirty men. Each of the women had a woven plaque in their hands. On that plaque was a heap of cornmeal that was packed tight. There was a hole in its center and around that hole were two rings, one of red hematite and one of yellow hematite. Actually, that yellow stuff may have been something connected with uranium. *Uranium was rediscovered several years ago to the west of Hopi Land.*

A flame was coming out of the hole in the plaque. When the flame goes down into the hole the explosion would occur. But before that could occur, a group of men and the women carrying the plaques came up through the cliffs on the west side of the village. The women put their plaques down in a circle on the plaza. The chief was given one such plaque. He accepted it and took it into his home to bless it. Then he left to catch up with those of his people who had left early. And the women and men who performed the ceremony came with him.

Those who did not believe the warning remained in the village to see what would happen. A big explosion and intense heat blasted the moment the flames went down into the hole on the ceremonial plaques. The people who remained died. The whole village was destroyed. Even some of the people who had left early were affected by the heat and had to be carried by others.

The survivors could not go to Oraibi because their time had not come yet. They could only come to Oraibi at a specified time that was determined by their Kachinas. The Forehead Clan continued its migration. Later, this clan was accepted in Oraibi – as the last of the three Fire Clans.

The fiery event at Huck'ovi took place more than 3,000 years ago. We still have a song about it. That song does not mention the reason why Huck'ovi was destroyed but we sing only about what happened after the explosion. I will tell you later what it means but first hear the song:

It has been decided
that this would happen,
it will have to be ...

your houses will be covered
with red billowing flames
from village to village
they will run for safety
the survivors from the village
that was destroyed ...

It has been decided
that this would happen
it will have to be ...

Hee-a hee-a hee-a (the sobbing of children)
the children will be carried
on the backs of their fathers
who are looking for safety
in other villages
but they will find none ...

This song is sung in connection with the Huck'ovi legend but it is meant as a prediction and warning of what is going to happen to the whole world.

Here in our area only that one village was destroyed, and all those people who had left in time were saved. But the song tells you that people (those who survive), will go to the next village- and the next- and the next- for safety: *but they will find none* because everything will be burning.

There is no help anywhere.

This is the fire that will destroy our Fourth World: it is not caused by atomic warfare. This comes from an electrical weapon that today's scientists are developing. You can't stop them from doing it. I don't know how it works but it's something like sending radio waves from a radio station; it goes everywhere.

[Editor's note: Later, in White Bear's script he tells us, if we change our ways, our personal consciousness, and if we collect with others in communities that practice Creator's Law, the emphasis will be on what we are migrating toward rather than what is being destroyed.]

Arrival of the Spaniards in Oraibi

When the Kachinas left us ...

We were told to remember that one day people would come to our country from another land, and bring us knowledge of another faith.

My fathers of the Bear Clan were given a 7-foot long stick. On this stick they were to mark time. The stick was painted black and every year at the time of *Soyal* it was marked with a white line. The people of another country were supposed to arrive the very year when our stick was covered with marks all over its length.

The Kachinas told us that we were to meet these newcomers at a place called *Kowauayna* which is located on the *Rio Grande* about 30 miles North of Albuquerque, New Mexico. A big ruin still stands there today. In it is a large beautiful painting, part of which I copied for the *Book Of The Hopi*.

We were told if the strangers did not come during that year we were to mark another five years on a new stick, and the meeting place would then be at *Sikia'ova* which means *Yellow Stone*. This place is near the foot of the old road that leads up to Oraibi. If they had not arrived by then, we were to mark another five years and then we would meet them at a spot farther up that road, which is called *Chiwauchrha*, meaning *Hardened Clay* because there is a certain kind of adobe there.

After marking another five years we were to meet them at a place called *Cross Fields – Nahauangowasha*. Cotton and beans were raised in that area. There were arguments over the fact that people often went across the borderlines of these fields – therefore "cross fields."

And as a last resort a place at the upper edge of the cliff east of Oraibi was designated for a meeting after another five years. The name of that place is *Taotooma*.

The newcomers did not arrive when the first stick was full. Five more years went by and they did not come then. That went on, one five year period after another.

According to tradition, the ones who were supposed to come should have been brought to our continent by *Pahama, the Brother*. The word *Pahu* means *water*, but we don't have to say it fully, we abbreviate and say only *pa*. The *ha* means to travel by water, by boat. *Pahama* means therefore, *The Man who comes across the Water by Boat*. We knew (thousands of years before it happened), that they would come by boat, not by Flying Shields.

[Editor's note: A worthy read is the book, *He Walked The Americas* by L. Taylor Hansen. The book references a Master who came to tribal peoples to teach them the ways of peace. He came by water and often with twelve associates.]

Year after year, nobody came! Our people became concerned. They began to wonder. The long delay might mean that those expected were not the right people. Finally, twenty years late, "they" arrived and we prepared to meet them at Taotooma as we had been told.

You will remember that Taotooma was also the name of the area that had come up from the ocean, the place that was the first to be *touched by the arm of the sun*.

So, these strangers came to a place which had the same name. A long time ago that name meant a new beginning for us. *It would mean a new beginning now.*

As I said, my people were greatly disturbed about the twenty years' delay. The corn meal line was drawn when the Spaniards came. Our elders and religious leaders were there to greet the Spaniards. These strangers were in armor and had weapons, but we were not afraid because we still considered them as the Brothers, as cultured people.

But then tragedy struck! The chief of Oraibi extended his hand so that a *nakwach* could be formed, the symbol of true brotherhood. If the man on the other side would understand that gesture and symbol, everything would be alright. But when the Hopi extended his hand to the priest, the priest thought he was asking for a gift and he put a trinket into the chief's hand.

[Editors note: Nakwach is a symbol of Brotherhood – a type of handshake.]

This was a severe shock to the Hopi: the newcomers did not understand – they did not know the symbol of Brotherhood!

Our people realized then that from that moment on there would be trouble. Because the "others" did not show the symbol of Brotherhood to our chief, we knew that they were not the Brothers, and we knew there would be much sadness among the Hopi from then on.

And so it was.

We have witnessed it.

[Editor's note: The following is from an article that was printed in *Challenge Magazine,* Spring 1989. It is excerpted from the book, *Hopi: Songs of the Fourth World, A Resource Handbook, 1986* (for the film by Pat Ferrero).

The Hopi got their first glimpse of Europeans when Spanish soldiers entered their towns in 1541. In 1598, the king of Spain appointed Juan de Onate as his Chief Administrator. Onate's first policy regarding native populations came in the form of the "Act of Obedience and Vassalage." The date was November 1598. For the next eighty years the native people – Hopis included – were to learn the true meaning of the act. Incidents of enslavement, torture and punishment by death were legion throughout the Southwest.

In August of 1680 an all-out rebellion against the Spanish took place. Participants included the Taos to the north, the Isleta to the south, the Acoma, Laguna, Zuni and Hopi peoples also joined the effort. In the Hopi area the missions were destroyed and several missionaries and soldiers were killed. Spanish survivors retreated to the south.

By 1700 the Spaniards returned but Hopi warriors took back their land and that closed the final chapter of Spanish missionary activity of any consequence in the Hopi area.]

White Bear and Kaih

Part Five

Hopi Legend

Grandfather White Bear and "Noomer" as he called her.

White Bear and Kaih

Yucca Boy

There was a time when some of our clans still lived in *Palatupka*, the *Red Canyon* – now called *Canyon de Chelly*. The prominent clans living there before they came home to our Hopi villages were the Sun Clan, the Corn Clan and the Cloud Clan. Other clans living there were the Fire Clan and the Reed Clan; and there was a small clan which was little known at that time, the Yucca Clan. There were just a few people in that clan and they moved and settled together with the other clans. They established their homes in one of the side canyons.

A girl was born to a family in that small clan. When she grew up she became a very industrious and helpful girl who was liked by everybody. Then there was a big volcanic eruption somewhere far, far to the West, in a place they did not know. That eruption caused smoke to cover the sky and because of that there was no moisture – not a drop of rain for three years. Corn, beans, squash plants; everything dried up and died. Nothing grew and the people had to go out into the desert to search for things they could eat.

Everybody suffered.

The parents of the girl were too old to go out and so the girl who (was a young woman by then), went to search for food for all three of them. One day when she went out she filled her jar with water that came seeping out slowly from underneath a rock, and then she left. When she did not find enough on one day she would not go home but sleep somewhere and continue the next day.

During the third year food became so desperately scarce that the young woman had to go long distances in her search for food.

One day she decided to go out farther than ever to find an area where nobody else had been before. She wandered north towards the mountain. She wanted to bring home food that would last a few days. And so, for three days she continued to gather food here and there. Then she came to a beautiful spot lush with grain and dried berries that were still edible. Late in the afternoon she sat down and ate from the food she found.

There was a little hill nearby with a low cliff. She decided she would stay there overnight. While she was making her preparations she thought she heard something. She looked around but did not see any animals, so she went to sleep in the nice soft sand. She was warm because she had her cape and the blanket her father had made.

Early in the morning she decided that she had enough food now and that she would go home. Suddenly, she heard the sound she had heard the night before. She went up to the top of the little hill and from there she saw a stranger coming toward her. He was a very handsome young man, dressed in beautiful garments most delightful to look at.

Of course, her people had known Kachinas for a long time but it seemed that all the Spiritual People disappeared when the dark cloud came.

But now there was a stranger coming toward her. As he came closer she discovered what had made the sound she had heard last night and today. The man had shells strung across his breast and all over his body, shells from the ocean. And as he walked the shells hit one another making a noise.

She was not frightened at all. As he came closer she noticed how young and handsome he was. And from his

White Bear and Kaih

appearance she knew he had never lived under the conditions and the troubles she and her people were in now.

When he was close to her he said: "I see you have gathered enough food for your people." He had a very kind voice. Also, he seemed to know what he was talking about. So she said, "Yes, it was the first time I have gone out so far. I am glad I found all this food."

"I can understand that," he said. "We have been watching you. We know what happened." She was surprised and asked him where he came from.

The young man looked at her and said, "We are the Spiritual People, we do not dwell on this earth. We are from a planet far away but we do survey this country to which you belong. We are watching you," he said. "You will survive these hard times. What is happening now to your people is part of the change of conditions around the world."

The young woman was so surprised and she admired his appearance so much, that she could not ask more questions. So he said to her: "I know you cannot believe that where I come from everything is green and lovely." They sat down and she talked about her people and he talked about his. Their conversation was wonderful and time was passing fast. At one point the young man asked her, "You did not go back today, are you not worried about your people?"

"No," she said, "and it is so interesting to see someone like you, someone who is so well nourished." He answered, "I know you must be surprised. We don't generally eat your food. We live from the spirit that is in a food which is like your Snow Drop Dew. There is much of it in the universe." By now the woman believed the young man was one of the Spiritual People and she wished she could have some of this food that was supposed to be so abundant. Right away the young man asked her if she was hungry, and she said yes and that she would eat some of what she had gathered. "Oh, no," said the young man, "I brought something along for you," and he reached for a bundle made of buckskin which was tied to his hip. He opened it and to her great amazement he brought out what they had not had in a long time – dew pepper. This is sweet corn that had to be baked slowly in a pit overnight. Already the smell of it made her happy. He gave her one ear and told her to eat slowly, and she obeyed. "Later on you can have another one," he said.

They continued until it was almost dark and the young man said, "We will have a hard day of traveling tomorrow, so I think you and I had better stay right here for the night." Before they lay down he gave her another corn. She ate it and then they went to sleep.

He awakened her early the next morning and said, "It is time for you to go home. Your folks will be worried." The girl agreed and when she was ready to leave he gave her four ears of corn. He told her she could eat one during the day to remain strong, but that the other three must not be eaten before she got home.

Then she started her journey. The last time she saw him (from a distance), he was still standing on the hilltop. She hurried home to be with her parents again. How happy they were when she arrived. She showed them all the dry food she had gathered, which would last for a while. Then she showed her parents the special food, the three ears of corn, and told them what had happened. Her mother and father asked many questions about the stranger and the girl told them everything. They were all very happy.

Each of them had one ear of corn. The stranger had said the power of the food would not last long if they ate hurriedly.

So they ate very slowly and strength came back to their bodies.

But the parents were puzzled. They kept thinking about what their daughter had told them. They said nothing to other people about what had happened.

The young woman wanted to go out again and she hoped she would get some more corn. When the dry food she had gathered was all gone she went back to the hill and the young man was there again. Later she went out one more time. By then the hard winter was approaching, and everybody knew that food would be even more difficult to find.

When the two met for the third and last time, the stranger gave her a jar with seeds in it. He instructed her to keep it in the inner part of the house and to pour seed from the jar in complete darkness. Whatever seed fell out first was to be put in a basket, and then she was to leave the room. After a while, when she came back, she found the seed multiplied.

The young woman followed his instruction and it was amazing what she found every time she returned to the room. Sometimes she found beans, at other times there was corn or squash, and always a basketful. This jar (which we call the Holy Jar), kept the whole family supplied during the winter.

The family kept the Holy Jar a secret – not telling anyone what was happening. To keep the secret, the young woman went out and pretended to look for food.

Then at springtime she found out she was pregnant. This was surprising to her and she told her mother. The mother was worried about what to tell other people – especially who the father was.

The stranger was the only one the young woman had ever met and talked with. But there had been no relationship between them. The mother was puzzled more than ever and also a little ashamed, "How do we know who the person is who fathered the child?" One day the young woman said, "We could say I met a stranger and that we were together secretly." This was what they told the neighbors.

One morning when the dawn was brightest, the child came into this earth. It was a boy. The whole family was happy and accepted him. After the twentieth day the time for the washing of the baby's hair had come. This is an important event in a Hopi's life, and the family was worried because the father's parents are supposed to perform the ceremony. But who and where was the father?

Then the strangest thing happened. As the mother of the young woman was preparing to wash the hair herself, fog came into the canyon! This was the answer: the young man had said they were Spiritual People and that they were watching our land. Wherever there is the dew, the fog, the moisture, that is where the Spiritual People are. They had arrived to wash the child's hair!

There was no mother of the father to name the child so the mother's mother named him *Silicouche*. His mother was of the Yucca Clan and so they gave him the name of a Yucca plant which grows much taller than those we have here in our area.

The rains had come back and the people of the village no longer suffered from lack of food. The boy grew up beautifully. When he became a young man he told his mother that he wanted to go out on his own and hunt for game. His mother and grandparents provided him with food, a blanket, a bow and arrows.

He traveled north towards the mountain. On the third day he reached the foot of the mountain. There he succeeded in killing a deer. He cut up the meat to dry and preserve it, and he had a good meal for himself.

When he woke up early next morning he saw a stranger, a young man, standing by his game, and the stranger said to him, "So you have finally come to take your game." The stranger's voice was pleasant and Silicouche answered, "Yes, and this is the first time I am out hunting alone."

"Oh yes," said the stranger, "I know all about you."

Silicouche was surprised: "You know me?"

"Yes, I know you but the time has not come yet for you to know who I am."

The stranger then helped Silicouche hang the meat for drying. Towards evening when the meat was good and dry, they packed it into the skin of the deer. The stranger took the bundle on his back and told Silicouche to follow him.

He led Silicouche up the steep mountain. It was almost dark when they arrived on the top. There, on the mountaintop stood a building – just like our Kivas, only much larger. The stranger invited him in. Silicouche heard voices. When he came down the ladder into the kiva-like structure he saw a number of Kachina women and maidens sitting along the wall. Most of them were *Haha'ii*, the kindest of the Kachina women. He was welcomed in a very friendly manner, so he sat down in the middle of the room where the men were sitting.

A wonderful meal was served to him. And then the stranger said, "Now that you have come to our home, I can tell you: we are many People. We are all over this earth. I am your father." Silicouche could not say anything. There was his father and he was one of the Spiritual People!

He wondered why his mother and grandparents never told him who his father was. He often wondered, because all the other boys had fathers. Only Silicouche never knew.

His father continued to speak: "It is not time yet for you to know exactly who I am and what I am doing. You are a human being, you are not of us yet – but you will be one day. For now you are required to go through a trial: we will see if you survive."

Silicouche was very sad in his heart. Why in the world could his own father, when they had just met, put him to a severe test? But he knew he had to obey and said, "Yes, I will try."

His father led him to a high cliff that was quite some distance away on another mountain. While they were talking, Silicouche noticed for the first time his father was not really walking but was actually floating in the air just above the ground. He made motions of walking but he did not touch the ground.

"Here," he said when they arrived at the cliff. "This is the place where I will leave you. Have your bow, your arrows and your knife ready; you will stay here for the night."

Before Silicouche knew it, his father was gone – he just disappeared.

The young man (not knowing what to expect), climbed up to the top of the cliff. It was a difficult climb but he had made a good choice. For, as soon as it was completely dark he could hear the voices of dangerous animals. The animal's cries came nearer and nearer. It felt like hundreds

White Bear and Kaih

of lions, wolves (and any other animal that could tear a man to pieces), were trying to climb up to him. He was ready to defend himself, but the rock was smooth (he had a hard time climbing up there), so he was confident animals could not reach him. But he was very frightened. Where was his father? He did not sleep all night.

The roar of animals quieted down toward morning and when the sun came up there wasn't one animal in sight. He closed his eyes for a few moments and when he opened them again, there was his father right beside him.

"I see you made the wise decision to climb up here. You have survived. Now you can rest so that you will be ready for the next trial tonight."

They climbed down and sat at the foot of the cliff. His father gave him freshly made food of the same kind the Haha'ii mothers had prepared for him last night. Silicouche enjoyed it, and when he had eaten enough, he put his weapons close to him to be prepared and fell asleep.

There were no animals to disturb him now. Shortly before sunset his father returned. "Well, here you are," he said, "You will stay here again tonight. Make a good choice," and left him. The young man wondered, he had survived the first night with all the animals, but what could the second night bring? He walked around a little bit and then decided: "If this rock protected me during the first night, why should it not also protect me again?"

Darkness was approaching fast and as Silicouche looked at the steep rock, the only thing he saw that could be of some use was a small and shallow cave halfway up the cliff. He climbed up to it and found it a most uncomfortable place. In addition, if the animals would indeed come again, they could easily get to him this time. But it was now almost dark, and he had no other choice, so he stayed there.

The darkness of the night was heavy – then the storm came! Lightning struck with horrible fury and the thunder was deafening as it bounced off the rock cliff. It was by far the most terrifying storm he had ever experienced. The cave was too small to hide in so he clung to a slippery narrow rock ledge. If he slipped and fell down the cliff he would surely be killed – so he hung there all night. Toward morning he thought he could not go on. But somehow he managed to hold his body suspended on the rock ledge near the little cave.

After what seemed to be an eternity morning came, the storm subsided and his father appeared again. "Come down young man. My son, you have again made a good choice. This storm is my own element and I know therefore that you selected a good place to protect yourself."

"Now there is one more test you must go through." The young man was sad: why did his father punish him so hard? But he told himself that this was his father and that he had to obey. As the day before, Silicouche was served wonderful food and then he fell asleep immediately.

Sometime in the afternoon he was awakened by his father: "We have to walk a while to the place where you will face your last trial." They walked fast and for quite some time. They walked together until they came to a big mountain which was covered by a forest of big pine trees. "This is the right place," said his father, "Now prepare yourself."

Silicouche looked around. There were no rocks or cliffs any more but only trees, big beautiful trees. He thought for a while about what he should do and decided then that a tree would be the only place where he could be. He selected one and climbed up almost to its top where he could sit on a branch and put his arms around the trunk and lock his hands.

Night came and with it another storm. If possible at all, this storm was worse than that of the night before. The pine tree swung back and fourth wildly – as if trying to shake him off. He thought the night would never end. But the storm was over before morning, and when the sun came up he was happy as he heard his father say: "Come down, son, you have passed all your tests."

With what little strength he had left Silicouche climbed down to where his father stood. "I was hoping all the time that you, my son, would survive. I used my own power to test you. You have endured all this punishment and now I know that you are strong. You must be strong because there is much hardship for your people in the future."

Together they went back to the Kiva where they had been the first night. Silicouche was welcomed with great warmth because he (a human being), had gone through the tests and passed them all. Everything seemed much more pleasant to him now – after those terrible nights. He had wonderful food and afterward many Kachinas joined him. They sang and danced for him. They celebrated his survival and they blessed him because he had come through some very terrifying initiations. Yes, he was initiated now! While the Kachinas were still dancing, Silicouche happily fell asleep.

He woke up refreshed the next morning. His father came to him and said: "I have done my morning work already. I have blessed the earth with dew all over the land. Now we can go: your mother and grandparents will be worried because they do not know where you are and what happened to you." Silicouche was given food by the

Kachinas and then he followed his father up the ladder out of the Kiva.

His father told him, "I will help you part of the way home but I cannot go there with you. I cannot live with your mother and grandparents, but when I come as a fog, or as dew, you will know that I am there." Then he picked up the bundle of dry meat and they went on their way.

When they came close to Silicouche's home his father said, "From this point you have to go alone. When you get home tell your mother and grandparents that you have met your father. And tell them what they already know: that I cannot live with you because I am of a different world."

Silicouche tried to lift the bundle of meat and gifts from the Kachinas, but it was so heavy that he could not bring it up to his shoulder. "That is too heavy for you," said his father (who had easily carried it up to this point), "I will help you carry your bundle but you will not see me." With his father's help, Silicouche could lift the bundle and carry it – his father had become invisible.

When Silicouche got home all were happy – they welcomed him when he arrived. When his mother saw how much meat he brought she gave some of it away to their neighbors immediately.

Silicouche told them he had met his father. And he talked about the terrifying trials he had gone through. He repeated what his father had said: that he had to suffer to prove and increase his strength because there would be hard times in the future for all their people.

If he did not abuse the knowledge his father had given him, Silicouche, would become a custodian, a leader of a planet in his future life. He told them he had learned his father's name was *Hololo*, and that his father was a high warrior

Kachina, a Deity who had come from a far away planet. When he described his father, what he looked like and how handsome and strong he was, his mother recognized Hololo as the young man she met so many years ago. There was other information that was very important. His father had told him that when he met his mother out by the hill three times, there had been no physical contact between them – confirmation of what his mother had told her parents from the beginning.

For many years whenever fog came into the canyon the people said that Hololo, the father of Silicouche, was coming. And many of us still call Canyon de Chelly the Fog Canyon.

Silicouche became an important leader. His gifts were a great help to his people. He could foretell when rains would come, how much snow there would be, when to plant and how to store the food they harvested. This was a gift from his father Hololo, a Kachina of the Cloud Clan people. He appears at the Mixed Dance at nighttime.

This is the end of the story of Silicouche who was born in the Red Canyon which is now called Canyon de Chelly.

[Editor's note: Located in northeastern Arizona, North America, Canyon de Chelly is a National Monument that was established as a unit of the National Park Service in 1931. Today, these ancient lands sustain a community of Navajo people who have deep-rooted historical and spiritual connections to this landscape, its architecture and artifacts.]

Part Six

The Hopi Point of View

Grandfather White Bear at his final birthday party.

About Energy

In Kasskara (Lemuria), all the power and energy we needed came to us from the sun. We could tap energy anywhere – and we did not need power lines. But I don't know how it was accomplished.

We had an object (many of them actually), with a crystal in it that was only about one inch big. At that time people did not have to chisel away on a rock day after day. They only had to hold this instrument in a certain way. The sun was reflected in that crystal and then they could cut any stone, with the power of the sun.

Also, all sounds were recorded in crystals. All records of the Third World are stored in a cave somewhere in South America. My grandmother told me that. She also said that nobody knows where that cave is anymore. But if ever that cave is found I could identify everything in it. Such objects and our knowledge were of course brought to this continent when we migrated over here.

Down in South America our people could lift gigantic rocks by just holding out their hands; they did not have to touch them. Others are amazed and puzzled by how we built our great cities. At that time it was simple.

The highest potential of a man's abilities are in his fingers. There is so much power that radiates from them – and what wonders the fingers in a person's hands can receive!

A medicine man puts his fingers on your body to feel its vibrations. He can feel the good vibrations and he feels vibrations that should not be there. In this way he finds where ailments are.

At one time the ancients used mercury but I am not sure what it was used for. According to the Hopi it comes in two types: one is solid and one is liquid. Somehow it seems to be connected with heat and with balancing. I don't know if that means anything to you, scientifically? The Two-Horn People used it. I heard that from a Bow Clan man.

The ancients were very technical but they did not use their power to destroy human lives. The ancient knowledge was gradually lost and the people had to work much harder because of that loss. Today all those good things are hidden from us, and we look at what was done in those ancient times with amazement. Compared with the ancients, one might say we live in the dark ages.

White Bear and Kaih

About Symbols

After our arrival and as our people settled in South America, we began to document our presence. We expressed our spiritual and historical knowledge through symbols. We still do today. We inherited these symbols from our fathers and we know the meaning of the figures and lines. We know what they stand for. There is something behind these symbols that is expressed through them.

We have left our documents wherever we lived and migrated. The symbols, the evidence of our knowledge and our presence can be found almost everywhere from Easter Island, to South America and up to the North American continent. The rock writings, the pottery and the buildings – this is evidence of our presence. There are people who say we don't have a written language! Yet there it is – this is our writing and our message is written all over several big continents. Our message still exists; it has yet to be destroyed.

We have etched our symbols on rock because rock cannot be easily destroyed by weather. We have decorated our pottery with symbols, and we still do today. During our migrations, whenever we left an area where we had settled for a number of years, the children would go out and break the decorated pottery and scatter it all around the village. Pottery cannot be destroyed. It can break alright but the shards will remain forever. When other groups and younger generations come and find the shards they know we were there before them.

Then there are the buildings, the ruins; you will again find them all the way from South America to North America. But here you have to look for certain specific things – then you may understand. In the ruins of the old buildings there are the towers – for instance, the round tower. The round tower symbolizes the female, the square the male.

And there is the so-called keyhole shape, or T-shape. That is very important and has been with us since the First World. That shape represents the plan of the Creator. For that reason the floor plan of our Kivas is in the T-shape.

And while I speak about Kivas, I will mention other symbolic meanings in their structure. The lower floor represents the First World, the raised upper floor the Second and the whole part from back to front represents the Third World. Then there is a raised platform on the flat roof of the Kiva, which represents our present Fourth World. Now, perhaps you will understand why Kivas are so important to us.

Our symbolism and knowledge is expressed in the great buildings of the past. The three previous Worlds, plus our present Fourth, the Fifth, Sixth and the Seventh Worlds mankind has yet to go through – are referred to everywhere. Evidence is in the number of steps of the pyramids, in the number of doors of the buildings at their tops – it's there. Also the Nine Worlds are recorded, including the two Worlds that belong to the Creator. The evidence is there in the sculptures and even in the arrangement of buildings! I could write another book about the meaning of things in the ruins of Central America and Mexico.

There is meaning everywhere – and our history is documented everywhere. We are spiritually-oriented people and archaeologists and historians must comprehend that. *They must come to understand our people before they can understand the ruins.*

White Bear and Kaih

In the present time we carry these symbolic figures with us, or rather *in* us. No longer in material form but in much more subtle ways. For instance, when the kachina dancers perform in the plaza, they make their formation in only three places. This indicates the three worlds we have gone through. They cannot form their groups four times because our Fourth World is not complete yet.

And I must mention the songs we sing during ceremonies. Such a song tells us that we will emerge to the Fifth World – *for it has five stanzas.*

That shows you that the Hopi know exactly where we are in the big world plan. We are between the Third World that was destroyed and the Fifth which we will reach next.

We know that we are in this Fourth World and we know we are at the midway point of Seven Worlds – the truth of this is expressed symbolically in our ceremonies. What need is there to write down knowledge which is so firmly rooted and so clearly presented in our ceremonies?

The symbolism the Hopi uses today is a reminder of truths we learned long ago. But only we, the Hopi, know and understand our symbolism. No other tribe understands – although some of them are now using Hopi symbols. But they see only the surface, they lack the knowledge.

So, whenever you see our symbols, on Easter Island, in South America or Central America or on this northern continent, remember that we still have the knowledge of what the symbols tell us. And remember also, we inherited all our knowledge from the past – from our fathers. And remember – we are keeping it alive.

Remember too, Hopi knowledge goes further than what I have spoken of here. We have also written with our voices (and without sound), into the atmosphere. And that is indestructible! Rocks and ruins will eventually be destroyed. But what we say and what our minds are thinking on a higher universal plane – that can never be destroyed.

A Final Word

Every one of us is born with an assignment ...

And we have to fulfill our destiny in this world. Long before I was conceived it was determined that my destiny is to record all these things. And this is why I have come to talk to you.

[Editor's note: The script from which this book was taken originated by recording White Bear's voice on a tape recorder. His wife Grandmother Naomi typed the original script.]

Very early in these tape recordings I told you the history of my people. My words are coming to you with a warning. I hope you have understood by now what that warning is.

Did you notice how history repeats itself again and again and again? And do you see that the Creator punishes mankind when they violate His Laws, and get away from the true path?

I have told you much about our history, the history of the chosen people. I know it is different from what you have previously known. Of course, the Hopi will be reprimanded by scientists, they always are. They don't understand us, and so they cannot understand our history and our insights.

But we Hopi recognize (in the events of current times), the same things that happened towards the end of the Third World are now repeating. We see what goes on in this world now, the corruption, the killings, and we know that the world is right on course with its own destruction.

We can avoid the terrible end if we honestly return to the true path of the Creator!

But I fear this will not happen. The next great catastrophe is not far away, only a few years. That may all sound strange to you in your world; but we know.

We Hopi know.

Epilogue

Wrapping it up ...

As White Bear said, "Every one of us is born with an assignment." Obviously one of my life assignments has been to bring "Bear's" final earthly project out to the reading public.

The task of making this book available (while daunting), has been a work of love – a gift to my long gone friend – White Bear. My efforts are devoted to the Hopi Nation, and to curious explorers of truth and history everywhere.

I am not an expert on Hopi history, and the Hopi way of life, so Editor's notes for clarity were all that was added to the original script.

The History of the Hopi from Their Origins in Lemuria contains warnings of impending disaster relative to the global conditions in today's world. According to White Bear, there are Nine Worlds that mankind will ultimately experience, and each of the Higher Worlds open to those who have expressed compassion and obedience in their lives – but only following the destruction of a previous World.

The Hopi Prophecy may simply be saying, be good to your neighbor, stop arguing and warring against one another. Be the best person you can be – or suffer the consequences.

It is my contention that we all have the *potential* to be *people of peace* and yet the same dangerous behavior has plagued mankind from our very beginnings.

Humankind is composed of many kinds of people, all created by God to please God. We are fields of wild flowers of variant colors, fragrances and forms and we all contribute to and take from God's Meadow. If our diversity pleases God then we must be designed diversely for our own pleasure.

As Grandmother Naomi tells it, "It is the dark and the light in our nature not the shades of our skin that counts." And our many religions and spiritual practices, our various languages, the foods and smells we respond to, and our differing family practices should bring us happiness not suspicion.

In the past, it has been mankind's practice to take sides against each other, to create war, to steal the goods of others and to ignore suffering; all in the name of peace. It has never worked and it never will.

So here we are, right where we have been before – cliff hanging – on the edge – at the end.

The things that are destroyed at the end of an age are selfishness, foolishness and ignorance. They are destroyed! So why has mankind continued to recreate (from age to age), the very things that caused us misery in the past?

A new beginning is being offered to us. The question remains, can we participate in a better kind of life in the Fifth World and let the past rest in peace? Can we fail on one vital point this time? Can we fail to repeat the lessons of the past by simply loving our existence so much that we admire, treasure and encourage every other person who also lives on this sweet Earth? In the Fifth World, will we build a Divine society rather than cathedrals, mosques, banks and monuments to our egos?

Can we drop tribal pride and replace it with appreciation for another person's (or nation's), skills and recognize the beauty of other cultures and traditions?

And the biggest question of all is, "Will we love each other?"

White Bear told me, the world is shaped by two kinds of people – those who hold to Creator's Law, caring for each other, educating themselves in spiritual ideals – and there are those who are destructive.

But is that premise written in stone? Do so-called spiritual people also cause destruction? If we create envy by having more than our neighbor, if we create jealousy by flaunting riches in the face of ones who have not and know not, if we create less for others to gain more for ourselves, then what may be seemingly spiritual is ignorant at its core. And such ignorance can only generate destruction.

So we are best advised to prepare Heavenly Consciousness *before* we exit this Fourth World. If we do, we will accomplish humanity's highest goal – to fail to repeat the mistakes of our yesterdays.

We have the opportunity to shift the Fourth World into the Fifth (for worldwide populations), by being and living the Golden Rule: Love each other as I love you! And by changing our minds, by lifting our thoughts, by activating our brains, opening up our DNA/RNA and "Doing It", we can make every moment an era, an age of peace and plenty!

White Bear says, we must exit the Fourth World and its chaos and migrate into the Fifth World of higher consciousness where Divine Order is available to those who are willing to partake. But why wait for some shocking thing to occur? Why not be God's consciousness expressing God's will, right here – right now – and enjoy the freedom this brings?

The destruction of the Worlds and the entrance into Higher Worlds could relate to the evolution and civilization of humankind. Moving into the Fifth World can be like trading in a way of life that no longer supports well-being, for lifestyles that enrich, enhance and beautify *any* World we experience.

From the First World, to the one we live in today, we see the same problems repeated. The worldwide dilemma we see today is caused by pride, self-centeredness, greed and the desire to empower one's self over others. Those qualities destroy.

Humanity is called by the Creator to *create*. "Go out and be fruitful. Move up into the Fifth World now. Don't hang around to see the circus tents go down. Look into beauty. Live in kind rapport with other creatures and Mother Earth. Stimulate your body by thinking bright thoughts. Praise and encourage each other and be generous. The more we give away the more that comes our way. And this time let it stay that way."

The Migration into the Fifth World is upon us – and living there must be via the Spiritual Path.

Perhaps, if we set aside those things we have no power to change, and focus on the good we can do in this lifetime, the Fifth World will appear on its own – and the past will be just that – the past – gone!

Kaih Khristé King

Bibliography

Challenge Magazine, Torrance, CA, Spring 1989

Edith A. Folb, Ph.D., Editor, *Songs of the Fourth World, A Resource Handbook,* (for the film by Pat Ferrero)

Frank Waters, *Book of the Hopi*, Viking Press, 1963